The approximate locations of the hikes listed below are shown by the circled numbers on the map on the facing page.

At the back of the book are: an alphabetical list of hikes and variations; tables grouping trips by length and by appropriate time of year; and an index to available maps.

100 HIKES
IN WESTERN WASHINGTON

Hike Descriptions by Louise B. Marshall
Photographs by Bob and Ira Spring
Sketch Maps by Marge Mueller

THE MOUNTAINEERS • SEATTLE

THE MOUNTAINEERS
Organized 1906

To explore and study the mountains, forests, and watercourses of the Northwest;

To gather into permanent form the history and traditions of this region;

To preserve by the encouragement of protective legislation or otherwise the natural beauty of Northwest America;

To make expeditions into these regions in fulfillment of the above purposes;

To encourage a spirit of good fellowship among all lovers of outdoor life.

Fifth Printing, August 1968

Copyright© 1966
The Mountaineers, Seattle, Washington 98111
P.O. Box 122

Manufactured in the United States of America by
Craftsman Press, Inc.
Seattle, Washington

Library of Congress Catalog Card No. 66-25080

Photo on cover:
Eldorado Peak from Cascade Pass—Hike 80

Photo opposite title page:
Goat Mountain and Mount Shuksan from Winchester Mountain Trail—Hike 86

FOREWORD

"Sunday, February 17, was the date of The Mountaineers' first local outing. Promptly at 9:30 a.m. forty-eight members and their guests made the start for Fort Lawton. At the fort they were met by Captain H. A. Smith, who gave them a cordial welcome; from there a brief walk through the woods brought the party to the West Point light house, where they were greeted by the light house keeper, Mr. Thomas, and his family. Here a camp-fire was made and luncheon eaten. The return was made at low tide by way of the beach to give those interested in marine life an opportunity to gather specimens."

Thus did the March 1907 issue of **The Mountaineer** describe the first trip sponsored by the new organization. The second outing "included a trip to Lake Washington, from there to Kirkland by boat, with a seven-mile tramp along the belt-line road." During a hike to American Lake, "one ornithologist listed thirty-four birds seen in the ten miles traversed." The spring season climaxed in early May with an ascent of Mount Si, the party leaving Seattle Friday evening in a railroad baggage car, returning Monday morning "all sunburned, triumphant and loyal to Mount Si or 'Mount Sigh' as some now wish to call it."

All this, of course, was largely by way of preparation for an extended expedition into the largely unknown center of the Olympic Mountains that summer, during which the first ascent of Mount Olympus was made. However, there was good fun in the preparation, too. "Local Walks," as they were then called, proved as important to the club as the more ambitious and adventurous "Summer Outings" during those early years when the railroads, streetcars, and mosquito fleet were the usual means of travel to the edge of wilderness.

In following decades, as it became possible to reach high mountains on a weekend or even a single day, Local Walks grew into the more comprehensive "Trail Trips" extending from saltwater beaches and lowland forests in winter to alpine meadows and summits in summer—something going on, someplace to walk, the year around. Later other club units were formed, the Climbers, the Viewfinders, and the Campcrafters, to sponsor other sorts of hikes, on and off trails.

The experience gained in the past 60 years, on many thousands of outings by many thousands of Mountaineers, is the background of this book; the reason for this book is to share some of that experience with the broader community of valley-pounders, ridgerunners, and hillwalkers beyond the current membership of The Mountaineers.

Emphasis must be placed on the "some": the 100 hikes described here were selected from a preliminary list of several hundred, a list which in itself was by no means a full compilation of all the outings Mountaineers have taken and enjoyed and would recommend to others. Initially the Literary Fund Committee (which directs publication of Mountaineer books) felt that not even rough justice could be done the beaches, forests, and mountains of Western Washington with less than 200 hikes; the decision to proceed with half that number was forced, really, by the urgent need to relieve pressure on individual club members who have found themselves spending an increasing amount of time providing new arrivals in the Northwest—and new converts to the sport of walking—with sketch maps showing the start of the Mount Si trail, suggestions on "good places to see a glacier" and "what can you do around here in winter if you don't ski?"

If this book finds acceptance, The Mountaineers plan to publish others sharing still more of their experience. Meanwhile, though, the 100 trips recommended here (which with suggested variations total at least twice that number) should keep just about any walker busy and happy for several years; in fact, a lifetime would not be enough to experience every detail of these trips in all their varied moods. There are suggestions for every season of the year, for beaches, forests, rivers, lakes, meadows, and summits, for short afternoons and full weeks, for the Olympics from the Pacific Ocean to Hood Canal, for the Cascades from Mt. Adams and Mt. St. Helens to the Canadian border and from Puget Sound lowlands to the edge of the Columbia Plateau. In total, the following pages contain a representative sampling of the much larger riches that make Western Washington as good a hiking country, probably, as one could find anywhere.

Are Feet Obsolete?

A newcomer to the Northwest, or to hiking, is impressed by the extent and variety of the trail country and has trouble believing there is any serious threat to the future of pedestrian travel. However, those with the longer view provided by years or decades of walking local hills and valleys are worried; unless all hikers come to share this worry, and join together to take appropriate action, there will be steadily more to worry about as time goes on.

The American attitude toward feet is symbolically expressed by the fact that the Second Lake Washington Bridge, completed in 1964, was constructed without provision for pedestrians —unlike the first bridge, built 20 years earlier, and from the beginning a popular Sunday stroll, across the lake and back.

Selecting trips for this book sharply pointed up the problem. Though some excellent lowland walks were finally chosen, close to urban areas and suitable for the 5 or 6 months of the year when the high country is deep in snow, there was not much to choose from. Most of the recommendations follow roads—gated roads, to be sure, with very limited automobile traffic — simply because there are virtually no purely foot routes left in the lowlands. Some of the trips recommended here may very well have to be deleted in the next edition, wiped out by a new suburb or a new scenic drive.

There have been hopeful signs in the last year or two that progress may begin to take a new direction. Stimulated by the agitation of a citizen-action group, King County is now planning a path along Sammamish Slough designed solely for feet and bicycles. The Mountaineers, among other organizations, have urged public officials to plan a system of foot-and-bicycle trails throughout urban areas and their hinterland.

Beach walking, a Puget Sound tradition from the earliest days, may become a memory if the trend is not reversed. State of Washington law allows officials to sell the "land" between the levels of mean high tide and low tide to private parties, and because of this law few extended stretches of beach are technically open to the public—even if the public can reach the beach, no small problem in itself. Access to beaches is now being regained with funds recently voted by the people; by devoting some of these funds to repurchasing privately owned beaches or acquiring easement over them, tidewater walks could once more, and permanently, become a treasured amenity of life in Western Washington. The City of Seattle has undertaken such a program on the shores of Elliott Bay—encompassing, interestingly enough, the scene of the first outing by The Mountaineers, on February 17, 1907. The railroad lines extending along miles of beaches north and south of Seattle offer a relatively low-cost, low-effort opportunity for a foot-and-bicycle path possibly without parallel in the United States.

Beyond the lowlands, in the front range of the Cascades, the trail shortage has become steadily more acute. Potential hikers swarm out from Seattle on a sunny Sunday in March. By the hundreds they find the Mount Si trail (solely by word of mouth before publication of this book, since it is unmarked); by the thousands they **don't** find the Si trail, or any other, and drive around highways and backroads looking into the deep snows of the high mountains, and the trail-less brush and forests of the low valleys and hills.

The North Bend area is a prime example of undeveloped hiking opportunities. Little Si, Fuller Mountain, Rattlesnake Ledge, Herpicide Spire—each of these, given a trail and a listing on a prominent recreational signboard map erected at a strategic highway turnout, would attract many of the thousands who come looking for a hike, and don't find it. The crowds on Big Si suggest that similar trails to its neighboring peaks, Green and Teneriffe and Washington, might carry traffic loads as heavy as any in the Cascades.

The patchwork pattern of private and public land ownership, dating from the 19th century, has so far prevented any comprehensive development of trail systems in the foothills and front ranges, exactly where the closeness to population centers makes for the greatest demand. And in plain truth, no public agency has indicated any awareness of a problem—or an opportunity. Consideration should surely be given, by someone, to establishment of a Washington State Trail System that would supplement and in some cases tie into the systems of the National Forests and National Parks. Perhaps the State Parks Commission, until now preoccupied with recreation centered around automobiles and boats, could be assigned responsibility (and funds) for gaining easements over private ownerships and building and maintaining trails through the patchwork country; legislation has been introduced into Congress that would provide state agencies federal funds for planning such trails and for half the construction cost.

Are Foot Trails Obsolete?

The total amount of trail mileage has been drastically diminished in the past generation by new roads, including logging roads, but except in the lowlands and front ranges there is nothing approaching a shortage. However, a relatively new development, the scooter, threatens to convert the overwhelming majority of remaining trails into roads—narrow roads, but roads all the same, and distinctly not walking country in the traditional sense.

The scooter-rider, enclosed in his personal miasma of noise and fumes, is not bothered by the pollution, and like the man who has eaten garlic before attending the symphony, wonders why everyone is scowling at him. But very plainly the walker **is** bothered. Certain popular scooter

tracks have been virtually abandoned by pedestrians, driven out by the annoyance, or even the danger. Many hikers go to wildlands in the first place at least partly to escape from machines and all they symbolize; they do not find what they seek on trails that have become narrow-gauge highways.

As the reader will soon discover, many of the trips recommended in this book are flawed by scooters. National Parks are completely pure as a matter of Park Service policy, as are Wilderness Areas and Primitive Areas in National Forests by terms of the Wilderness Act. The Cascade Crest Trail and a few of its feeders are barred to mechanized travel by administrative ruling, as are some others, mostly too rough for wheels in any event. The deliberate decision was made **not** to mention the status of individual trails, there seeming little sense in a hiking guide serving the scooter-riders.

It must be said that scooters are fun, apparently. Quite obviously many, if not most, of those who ride mountain trails enjoy the raucous physical challenge, spiced with danger; that the sport happens to be conducted in areas of great natural beauty is a fortuitous circumstance—that's simply where the trails happen to be. But if scooters were barred from all trails, everywhere, the sport could easily thrive, in the lowlands and mountains both, on the hundreds and perhaps thousands of miles of low-grade logging roads and bulldozer tracks which are barely passable or not at all to automobiles, and as rough and sporty tracks as a rider could ask for.

Unfortunately, much of the fun seems to lie in taking machines where machines have never been before. Jeep-riders pit their four-wheel drive and winches against the unconquered open terrain of the east-slope Cascades. Amphibious swamp-buggies drive deep into unconquered marshes. Sand-buggies conquer the dunes. Hot-rods and even sedate family sedans splash along ocean beaches, conquering the surf. Snowmobiles seek to conquer the mountains in winter. And float planes land on alpine lakes, and helicopters flop down on high meadows. Every province of the wildlands is challenged with an appropriate mechanical ingenuity.

Moreover, just as pioneer motorists banded together to campaign for better roads, scooter clubs are agitating for smoother and wider trails, and for "equal rights" in Wilderness Areas and National Parks. And just as more and better roads engendered larger and more luxurious automobiles, the primitive chug-chug scooters are giving way to swifter models; three-wheelers and even four-wheelers are probing for opportunities, and manufacturers are developing enclosed passenger compartments to keep trail-drivers warm and dry.

To be sure, when America's trails have been converted into a system of little roads, the hiker will be allowed "equal rights"; scooter lobbyists self-righteously contrast their tolerance with the uncompromising attitude of pedestrians who say the sound and fury of machines have taken over so much of our world that **all** the quiet land remaining is just barely enough, that **no** mechanical devices should be allowed on **any** traditional foot trails **anywhere.**

Essentially, of course, it comes down to a matter of basic philosophy. If Americans decide to submit to the machine, then trail scooters are the wave of the future, pedestrians are anachronisms, and feet **are** obsolete.

Is Natural Beauty Obsolete?

To repeat, a newcomer to the Northwest, or to hiking, is typically too impressed by the grandeur and extent of mountain wilderness to be concerned about the nibblings he sees at the edges. And if he does find himself turning sick at the stomach amid ravaged forests and drowned valleys is likely to give a shrug of despair and say, "People have got to live. You can't fight progress."

The Mountaineers do not believe that progress necessarily implies total destruction and complete ugliness: to borrow a motto used by the Sierra Club, their policy is "Not blind opposition to progress, but opposition to blind progress."

The Mountaineers support all actions that improve the long-range health of the forest industry—including many things, such as planting unstocked tree-growing land and intensified research into the growing of trees and the full use of wood fiber, that are presently given lip service, but little more, by the industry. Similarly The Mountaineers want other resource-based segments of the local economy to thrive.

However, The Mountaineers are convinced that the long-range health of the local economy (resource-based and otherwise), as well as the long-range interests of people throughout the nation (who share ownership of the National Forests and National Parks), living and not yet born, demand that steps be taken to preserve some of the wildlands in the State of Washington.

High in priority is the creation of a North Cascades National Park which would set aside as a "museum of primitive America" a representative sample of forests, meadows, glaciers, and peaks. That the area is of National Park caliber is apparent to anyone who follows the routes described here for the Glacier Peak region and north. For the hiker, an important advantage of National Park protection over alternative land classifications is that guns are not allowed. The Mountaineers by no means oppose hunting, but do feel non-hunters should be allowed a "people refuge" in the North Cascades during the shooting season, which nowadays begins early in September, when much of the high country is at its best; many of the trips recommended in this book do not open to easy travel until the end of July, leaving only August available for walks free both of snow and guns.

The Mountaineers also urge the creation of several new Wilderness Areas, protected under terms of the Wilderness Act passed by Congress in 1964, with no logging, no mechanical contrivances, no roads, no permanent human structures, and no new mineral claims after 1984, set aside as areas where "the earth and its community of life are untrammeled by man, where man himself is a visitor who does not remain." Among the trips recommended here are many within the proposed North Cascades Wilderness, adjacent to the Canadian border; the existing Glacier Peak Wilderness; the proposed Alpine Lakes Wilderness north and east of Snoqualmie Pass; the proposed Cougar Lakes Wilderness east of Mount Rainier National Park; and the existing Goat Rocks and Mount Adams Wildernesses.

To adjoin and complement the North Cascades National Park, The Mountaineers urge creation of a transitional North Cascades National Recreation Area, saving the scenery of certain forests and meadows and lakes for recreation while allowing some uses, such as recreational roads, that are not permitted in Wilderness Areas, and others, such as hunting, that are not permitted in National Parks.

Elsewhere, Olympic National Park must be protected from the attempted timber raids that began shortly after establishment of the park in 1938, and have recently been renewed. Mount Rainier National Park should be enlarged to include **all** of Mount Rainier, not merely its glaciers and flowers.

Further, unwise hydroelectric and irrigation and flood-control projects must be blocked to save such wild rivers as remain for fishermen, kayakers, hikers, and all who enjoy free-flowing water. Saltwater beaches on the Pacific Ocean, Puget Sound, Hood Canal, Strait of Georgia, Admiralty Inlet, and Strait of Juan de Fuca must be saved for the public, rather than going universally into summer-home subdivisions.

This, in brief and partial summary, suggests the concern felt by The Mountaineers for the future of the "natural beauty of Northwest America." To protect that natural beauty, governmental action is required at the federal level, the state level, and the local level. To gain such action, the informed interest and active support of **every** citizen who values natural beauty is essential.

Individuals and organizations wishing further information about specific proposals for protection of wildlands are invited to write: Conservation Division, The Mountaineers.

About The Mountaineers

The Mountaineers, with groups based in Seattle, Everett, Tacoma, and Olympia, invite the membership of all lovers of outdoor life who sympathize with the purposes of the organization and wish to share in its activities.

Conservation education is a most important club responsibility and becoming more so each year. Preservation, though, is only one side of the coin; the other is using and enjoying wildlands.

The Mountaineers sponsor a year-round program of climbing, hiking, camping, ski-touring, and snowshoeing. Hundreds of outings are scheduled each year, ranging from single-day walks to trips lasting 2 weeks or more. On a typical weekend, as many as 20 or 30 excursions may be offered, from ocean beaches to the summit of Mount Rainier. In addition, members engage in countless privately organized trips of all kinds; perhaps a major value in belonging to an outdoor organization (The Mountaineers or any other) is the opportunity to meet other people with similar interest, to make new friends.

The Climbing Course, presented annually since 1935, with sections in Seattle, Everett, Tacoma, and Olympia, is the oldest and largest climbing school in America, and its textbook, **Mountaineering: The Freedom of the Hills,** has been adopted by virtually every other such school in North America, and by others in nations throughout the world. Each year, also, a Hiking and Camping Course is offered, and a Ski-Mountaineering Course. For further information on club activities and how to join, write: The Mountaineers, P.O. Box 122, Seattle, Washington 98111.

July, 1966   HARVEY MANNING

ACKNOWLEDGMENTS

Thanks are extended to the following Mountaineers (or just plain mountaineers) who helped gather trail information: Mildred Arnot, Donald B. Brannon, Don Brown, Bartlett Burns, Beatrice Buzzetti, Kenneth Carpenter, Ray Clift, Fred T. Darvill, Donna DeShazo, A. D. Fisken, Helen Gilmartin, Marjorie Gilmartin, Marjorie Goodman, Kenneth Hitchings, Ken Hunich, Vivian Joyce, Charles Hargraves, John Klos, Betty Lane, Philip and Pat Leuthy, Isabelle Lynn of the Double K Ranch, Harvey Manning, Ann Louise Marshall, George W. Martin, Mike McKeag, Tom Miller, Ted and Marge Mueller, John D. Rieman, Tina Rosen, Dorothy Sincock, Hans Smith, Robert B. Sperlin, Bob and Ira Spring (obviously), Dorothy Stapp, Helen Stoody, John Stout, David J. Swaney, Edwin A. Thompson, John F. Warth, and Robert L. Wood. Thanks also to the Washington State Department of Conservation, the Washington State Library, and the Bellingham Public Library.

Special gratitude is due the officials of the U.S. Forest Service, National Park Service, and Washington State Department of Natural Resources who checked the maps and descriptions for accuracy, and in more than one case took steps to improve routefinding aids (trail signs) in anticipation of publication.

The book was planned under the direction of the Literary Fund Committee: Burge Bickford, Donna DeShazo, Jack Hazle, Ward Irwin, Bob Latz, Tom Miller, Al Robinson, and Harvey Manning, chairman. Tom Miller served throughout as executive editor, responsible for putting words, maps, and photos together and turning them into a book. Harvey Manning assisted as copy editor.

Others helped in ways not easy to describe or even to remember. The primary debt is to the thousands of Mountaineers who have walked these trails since 1907 and led the makers of this book to walk them.

INTRODUCTION

Many readers need no introduction to the techniques and pleasures of walking hills and valleys and beaches, and probably have already skipped these pages on their way into the heart of the matter—the 100 suggested places to go.

Others, though, newer to foot travel, may wish a bit of basic training before attempting the longer and more complex trips here described. The ideal way to gain this training is by tagging along with more experienced companions. Beginners who lack friends willing and able to act as tutors should consider joining an outdoor club—to make friends, as well as to learn whatever the club has to teach. Most of the larger urban centers in Washington have one or more such organizations which invite the membership of all who share their interests.

With experienced companions or without, a basic textbook can be useful, perhaps indispensable. The recommendation here is **Mountaineering: The Freedom of the Hills,** a textbook not only for climbers but for hikers as well. The first section, "Approaching the Peaks," has chapters on equipment, camping, food and cookery, walking, and navigation. Following the sections on "Rock Climbing" and "Snow and Ice Climbing" comes "Safe Climbing," with chapters on leadership, mountain dangers, first aid, and rescue, and then "The Climbing Environment," covering geology, snowcraft, and weather.

Equipment

Some of the 100 trips in this book could quite literally be taken barefoot, naked, and hungry—and with any luck, in tolerable comfort and safety. Most of the trips, and most people, require at least a minimum of gear.

First (and last) come the feet. Tennis shoes are better than bare feet, but not much. Whenever the hike is longer than a leisurely afternoon, or crosses rough and rocky terrain, the only way to keep the feet in efficient operational condition is by wearing good-fitting boots with a leather upper 5 to 8 inches high and a rubber-lug sole, and within the boots, for warmth in cold weather and for cushioning in any weather, two pair of medium weight wool socks.

Proper clothing is necessary for comfort, perhaps even survival. Shorts and T-shirt are fine for a short walk in the sun, but in Northwest mountains the sun is chancy, cold storms never far away, and winter comes shortly after sundown. For long hikes, therefore, one should wear (or carry) lightweight wool pants and a wool shirt or sweater or both; for the high country, add a wool hat and mittens. Wool is emphasized, since it is warm even when wet. The garments needn't be stylish or new; old castoffs too disreputable for the city may have years of mountain life ahead.

To carry items essential for comfort or safety, including the clothing one must have along but may not want to wear while walking, a rucksack is necessary. Only a limited amount of gear can be carried in pockets or tied around the waist; an inexpensive rucksack with a reasonably spacious interior (don't bother with a skier's fanny-pack) immensely simplifies transport.

From years of experience, some of it tragic, The Mountaineers have developed a list of items that should be carried by every person on any trip more than a short stroll into the wilderness, items which provide the minimum conditions for survival when an accident or loss of route or sudden storm make the trip longer or more severe than expected. **Every** person should carry these "Ten Essentials," some in the pockets, some in the rucksack—which is why every person should have a rucksack.

1. Extra clothing. (Hike in shorts and T-shirt if desired, but be sure to have pants and shirt in rucksack and on high trips a sweater and perhaps a parka.)
2. Extra food. (The test: is there something left over at the end of the trip?)
3 Sunglasses. (In sunlight even a short snow crossing can be uncomfortably bright; extended snow travel without eye protection can do temporary or even permanent damage.)
4. Knife. (A simple pocket variety suffices; the main emergency uses are for first aid and splintering kindling for a fire.)
5. Matches. (Waterproof or in a waterproof container.)
6. Firestarter. (Solid chemical fuels, easy burning, for starting an emergency fire with wet wood.)
7. First aid kit. (Not only for serious injuries, but for possibly incapacitating miseries, such as blisters and heat cramps.)
8. Flashlight. (In good working condition, with fresh batteries and bulb.)
9. Map. (Of little value unless one knows how to read it.)
10. Compass. (Ditto.)

With boots, warm clothing, rucksack, and Ten Essentials, the hiker is basically equipped for a day's walk. To these may be added items desired for personal comfort, and perhaps a camera, not to forget food (in addition to the **extra** food). Overnight trips involve much more.

As important as knowing what equipment to carry is knowing where to buy it. In this respect hikers who live in Western Washington are exceptionally fortunate; firms located in the Seattle-Tacoma area are major suppliers to mountain travelers throughout the nation. An easy way to find such a supplier is to consult the Yellow Pages of the telephone book, under "Sporting Goods." It should be pointed out that most of the shops listed principally serve fishermen, hunters, car-campers, and skiers, and carry a limited, though often completely adequate, selection of hiking and backpacking gear. For the largest selections of American and imported equipment one should look for shops which in their name or advertising use such words or phrases as "recreational equipment," "alpine," "mountain," "climbers," "chalet," and the like.

Protecting Wildlands

Few of those who go into the hills actually prefer garbage dumps as a way of life, but many, through inexperience or thoughtlessness, help create a slum environment along the forest trails and in the alpine meadows. The techniques of "good mountainkeeping" are simple and mostly self-evident; the fundamentals mentioned here will suggest to any person of good sense a proper code of overall behavior.

The point has been abundantly made that it's not nice to burn down trees, and since nowadays virtually all forest fires are started by loggers and lightning, it is enough to repeat the familiar rules not to smoke while traveling and to be careful with campfires. What does require strong emphasis is that wherever possible, particularly in meadows, fires should be built on ashes left by previous campers. In virgin duff or heather a fire immediately kills several square feet or more of vegetation which will not regrow for years, and by unseen underground creep may destroy much more after the camper has left the scene. To avoid such destruction, and also to avoid the "logging" of alpine meadows, high-country hikers are rapidly abandoning the traditional wood fire in favor of lightweight backpacker stoves. Partly this is a matter of necessity; all the easy fuel has long since been gone from most popular alpine camps.

Meadows demand particularly tender loving care, not only in firebuilding but in every aspect of camping and sleeping and walking. Alpine heather, grass, and flowers **look** tough, and they **are** tough enough to withstand deer, goat, and marmots, but against man (especially when equipped with horses) they haven't got a chance —unless he walks softly, camps carefully. In heavily traveled areas one should always follow established trails to avoid converting still more of the green land to lanes of brown dirt. The recommendation of every authoritative camping manual (except **Freedom**) to "ditch tents in case of rain" must categorically and absolutely be condemned. Never, ever, gouge ravines in the greenery simply for the sake of a dry sleep; there are easier and kinder ways.

Trails can be wrecked by a relatively few horses or scooters simply by the act of passage, but hikers can't do much real damage unless they try. Unfortunately, some of those who rebel against modern city life by seeking out the wilderness fail to focus their rebellion accurately, and instead of venting their rage and frustration usefully (by writing letters to editors and Congressmen), vandalize the symbols of organized society they encounter along the wilderness way—the shooting up of trail signs (surrogates for the people or institutions they would like to shoot) being a common example.

Garbage is the major problem of popular hiking areas. If a hiker gives trails and camps the same consideration he does his house and yard, he automatically does the right thing by wilderness. Along the trail, he stuffs candy-bar wrappers and orange peels in his pockets or rucksack for later disposal. In camp, he burns all surplus paper and carries home, to city garbage cans, metal cans and wrappers, glass jars, and any other material fire cannot completely reduce to ashes. The old rule, when wildlands were virtually empty of people, was to burn tin cans, flatten them, and bury them along with the glass. Nowadays, though, digging a hole to bury garbage often merely excavates buried garbage. The new rule is this: **if you can carry it into the hills full, you can carry it out empty.** To follow the rule, the respectful camper now carries a large, heavy-duty plastic bag—a portable garbage can.

Another growing problem in the back country, where traditionally all water is completely pure, is described euphemistically as "random elimination", or "RE." Though little can be done about the personal habits of deer, much can be done about preventing horses from wading in Image Lake (to cite a loathsome example), and surely humans can take care of their needs at a distance from drainage channels. Sad to say, the water at some mountain camps (notably Cascade Pass) is so suspicious the camper may have to consider boiling.

Whenever a hiker encounters disgraceful conditions in the hills—shot-up or missing signs, trails or campgrounds being mangled by horses or scooters, garbage proliferating beyond tolerance, or any other situation incompatible with preserving natural conditions—he should report the problem, in person or by letter, to the government agency responsible for managing the area— usually the U.S. Forest Service or National Park Service. If a local ranger is not available, and one doesn't know how to contact a regional office, write to "U.S. Forest Service" or "National Park Service" in Washington, D.C. and the message will surely and certainly reach its proper destination—and ultimately be answered. Both agencies have exceptionally good reputations for sensitivity and responsiveness to citizen complaints and suggestions.

However, these federal agencies must not be blamed for all the barbarisms a hiker encounters in areas presumably under their jurisdiction. Much of the land that seems to lie within National Forests or National Parks actually is held by private owners. In the Central Cascades, particularly surrounding Snoqualmie Pass, the land is divided into a checkerboard pattern, some sections held by the people, others by individuals. Not all the logging of prime hiking country is the fault of the Forest Service; much is done by private parties accountable only to their own consciences and pocketbooks.

Miners continue to hold extraordinary rights and privileges in the public domain, granted by laws dating from the 19th century and revised only in minor detail since. The heartbreaking wasteland at the start of the Middle Fork Snoqualmie trail (on a patented mining claim), the jeep roads and junkyards near Windy Pass, the shanty town on Miners' Ridge, and many other high-country horrors are the fault of Congress, not the Forest Service.

You Can Go Home Again

Most hikers, when they set out on a trip, fully intend to return home safe and sound. Some don't make it.

The average new hiker perhaps need only be advised—**Take Care!** However, he may wonder how much care is sufficient and essential. The Mountaineers long ago found that to be the case, and after all too many climbers died from seemingly obvious blunders, adopted the following "Climbing Code," which has served beginning climbers well over the years. This set of rules is in most part equally applicable to hikers, and where not, defines the boundary between hiking country and climbing country.

A climbing party of three is the minimum, unless adequate prearranged support is available. On crevassed glaciers, two rope teams are recommended.

Carry at all times the clothing, food, and equipment necessary.

Rope up on all exposed places and for all glacier travel.

Keep the party together, and obey the leader or majority rule.

Never climb beyond your ability and knowledge.

Never let judgment be swayed by desire when choosing the route or turning back.

Leave the trip schedule with a responsible person.

Follow the precepts of sound mountaineering as set forth in Mountaineering: The Freedom of the Hills and other textbooks of recognized merit.

Behave at all times in a manner that will not reflect unfavorably upon our club or upon mountaineering.

H.M.

NOTE TO READERS:
YOUR CORRECTIONS AND SUGGESTIONS ARE INVITED

Probably the most infuriating thing in the world is a guidebook that misguides. The descriptions and maps here were prepared from reports based on the recent experience of numerous Mountaineers, were checked and double-checked by still more Mountaineers, and finally inspected by officials of the U.S. Forest Service and the National Park Service.

However, conditions sometimes change suddenly and without warning: streams wash out bridges and even entire sections of trails, blowdowns block easy paths with impassable jackstraws, a private owner abruptly logs off his land and in the process obliterates a 75-year-old route. Moreover, even the group memory of many hikers can be fallible, forgetting a confusing trail fork or remembering it wrong. Finally, history abundantly demonstrates that any guidebook must be proven through consumer field-testing to see if it actually does the job of getting people to the advertised destinations.

If **you** find this book useful, and would like to share in making future editions more useful, please make note of things you find wrong or misleading, or things you would like to see added or deleted or changed. Also, since similar books are planned if demand proves sufficient, please recommend hikes that might be included; a long preliminary list has already been drawn up, but your vote will be helpful in making a selection—and maybe you've been someplace the list-makers haven't but should.

Please send all corrections and suggestions to: Literary Fund Committee, The Mountaineers, P.O. Box 122, Seattle, Washington 98111.

1 TIGER MOUNTAIN

An easy road walk to a remarkable peak—tallest remnant of a mountain range older than the Olympics and Cascades, rising abruptly and high above impinging suburbs, with views from Rainier to Baker to the Olympics, down to foothills and villages and farms, and into Pugetopolis smog.

Drive on Highway 18—the Auburn-North Bend cut off—northeast from the Issaquah-Hobart road 3.3 miles; or drive southwest from U.S. 10 (from a point 3 miles east of Preston) 4.3 miles. Where the highway crosses a low but prominent divide, park in a huge bulldozed flat to the north. The gravel service road, completed in 1966, takes off from the parking lot. According to state plans, the road will be gated in most seasons, so cars ordinarily should be no bother; gates don't stop scooters, though.

The way is steep for 1½ miles, through cool second-growth firs and hemlocks and cedars, with the usual yellow violets and trillium and wild ginger and all, and several nice creeks in season. Rainier begins to emerge above ridges in the Cedar River Watershed. Then the road rounds a shoulder and enters a naked valley, relatively recently skinned of trees. The Olympics appear, and lowlands west, and also the summit lookout tower. After traversing the head of the naked valley, at 2½ miles is an intersection. Turn right and go ½ mile along a steep bleak hillside (interesting rock outcrops) to a saddle and an intersection with the older lookout road (from near Preston on U.S. 10). New views—from Rattlesnake to Si to Pilchuck to Glacier to Baker. Turn left for the final ½ mile (watch for a spring with dependable water) to the top. See everything seen before and more, and all at once.

The trip lies partly on state-owned land, partly on private land. In the next few years venturous suburbanites may be expected to build homes nearly to the summit. Now is the time for a magnificent Tiger Mountain State Park to be dedicated, with an ultimate network of foot trails and bridal paths. **Warning:** this is dangerous country during those autumn weeks when it's legal to shoot deer and people; the quality of the gunmen attracted is low. Experienced hunters won't go near Tiger on a dare. The best time for the walk is a sunny day in the dead of winter, when a little snow stops all wheels but is small hindrance to feet. For a spectacular view of city lights, carry water and a sleeping bag and camp on the summit.

Left from the 2½-mile intersection a road wanders 2 miles or so along the heights to West Tiger Mountain (airway beacon), which can also be deviously attained from the Issaquah-Hobart road, but that's another story.

Round trip 7 miles
Allow 5-6 hours
High point 3004 feet
Elevation gain 1644 feet
Best from late fall to early spring
One day

Lights of Seattle from Tiger Mountain

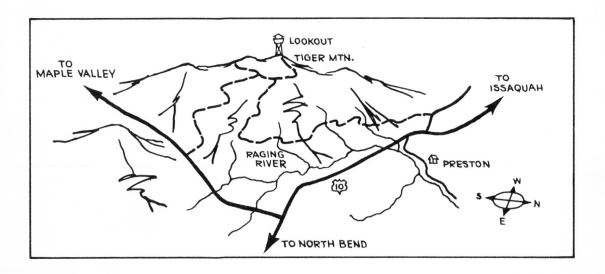

TO
MAPLE VALLEY

LOOKOUT
TIGER MTN.

TO
ISSAQUAH

RAGING
RIVER

PRESTON

10

W
S   N
E

TO NORTH BEND

2   MOUNT SI

Why is Si—monotonous, dry, and dangerous—nevertheless the most-climbed mountain in the state? Because it is close to the lowlands and strikingly prominent, its abrupt fault-scarp rising 3600 feet above the town of North Bend. Also, because many beginning hikers don't know better places to go. And to give the devil its due, because the views out over the Snoqualmie valley are superb.

Drive on US 10 east from North Bend, take the second left turn (432nd S.E.—Stilson Road), and cross the westbound lane of US 10. Then cross the Middle Fork of the Snoqualmie, keeping right beyond the bridge, and go about 1½ miles to a much-used parking area on the left, where the trail begins. This starting point is on private property, but the mountain itself and most of the trail are state-owned.

Recent improvements by the state have resulted in a clear trail that switchbacks easily up, passing an intermittent stream, the only water, at ¾ mile. A side trail to Little Si, at 2 miles, is easily recognized by its downhill course, the summit route being always uphill. The slopes of Si were swept by a great fire, or fires, in the last century or so, and thus have never tempted any logger. On the upper reaches the vegetation is even scrubbier, the trail stony, and the views inspiring.

Mt. Si should be treated with respect. There are no signs anywhere to indicate how to find the trail nor how to stay on it. Signs have been put up several times by the State Department of Natural Resources, but invariably have been destroyed or carried away almost as soon as installed. This is especially unfortunate since the shortcuts made by impatient travelers have confused innumerable hikers over the years. The absence of signs is also unfortunate because many hikers who didn't know there was a trail, or who couldn't find it, or who lost it, have come to grief on the rugged west scarp.

Haystack Basin, below the final pinnacle, is the proper turn-around point for hikers. The view from here is just as good as from the exact summit, and entails no risk to life or limb. The Haystack itself is easy for trained climbers, but a potential killer for those unfamiliar with rock techniques.

The south-facing, windswept trail side of Si is often mostly free of snow when all is white only a few miles east. Hikers are able even in January to walk at least partway up the mountain, far enough for worthwhile views down to the valley and across to Rattlesnake Ridge.

Round trip 10 miles
Allow 7 hours
High point 4190 feet
Elevation gain 3690 feet
Best March through November
One day

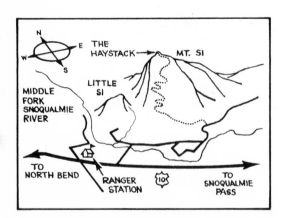

North Bend and Rattlesnake Ridge from Haystack Basin

3   McCLELLAN BUTTE

A miniature Matterhorn quickly reached from Seattle on the Snoqualmie Pass Highway. Fine views and interesting sights along the old trail, which is being cleared and maintained entirely by Boy Scouts of Troop #379, Highline District (Forest Service cooperating).

Drive on US 10 east from North Bend 11.3 miles to a very wide shoulder and a side road to Bandera. Turn right off US 10, cross bridge, park 50 feet beyond. To the right is a woods road, private property; walk along it 100 feet, turn left between two decrepit buildings onto National Forest land; follow an old wooden waterline going away from the highway and river.

Canteens can be filled where a fine log bridge, built by the Scouts, crosses Alice Creek. At 1/4 mile the trail intersects a powerline right-of-way, goes up it approximately 50 feet, then jogs left (no signs—look sharp) and continues parallel to Alice Creek. (Look back to see how the route will appear on the return.) The trail follows the old wooden pipe past beautiful creek scenes to a giant conduit issuing under a collapsing bridge. Here the old waterline had its beginning.

On private property again, the route crosses the Milwaukee Railroad track and then enters a vast cutover area where the trail has been totally destroyed. The Scouts have partially cleared a way through the slash, but this section is still confusing and unpleasant. Keep near (about 40 feet from) the edge of the creek gorge to find a path through the log carcasses to a fine forest trail. Shortly there are mining relics, an interesting cabin, and a mine shaft. (Not safe to enter.) At 1 mile the way crosses a logging road and re-enters National Forest land. A spring approximately 50 yards to the left along the road is the last water except for unreliable seasonal streams.

Above the logging road a few hundred feet there is a shaded rest spot where often a narrow stream burbles in a charming mossy dell. Rest is advised, for the next mile is steep, with no water and few views. At 2 1/2 miles a last switchback nears an open slope; rest a moment to look out over the valley to Mt. Defiance and Bandera Mountain. The next 1/2 mile heads south to attain the summit ridge at 4800 feet; from here there are fine views, including the seldom-seen (by ordinary citizens) Cedar River Watershed. At this point the trail enters the watershed for approximately 300 yards.

The final 1/2 mile goes northerly along a shelf on the west face of the ridge. From a fine campsite near a small pond, on a clear day one can see Lake Sammamish, Lake Washington, and Puget Sound, and in the evening watch the sun set behind the Olympics. A panorama from the summit includes Mount Baker and Glacier Peak to the north and a direct view into Willis Wall on Mount Rainier to the south.

Round trip 10 miles
Allow 7 hours
High point 5162 feet
Elevation gain 3962 feet
Best July through October
One day

Snoqualmie Pass Highway from the summit ridge of McClellan Butte

4   ANNETTE LAKE

A scenic little lake set in a crescent of cliffs. Good trail through dense forest all the way.

Drive east on U.S. 10 from North Bend about 17½ miles; turn south into the Asahel Curtis Nature Trail parking area. It is important not to miss this sudden turnoff; for the next 4 miles—clear to the summit of Snoqualmie Pass—there is no legal or safe place to turn around. The turnoff is about ½ mile west of a small sign, "Denny Creek", and exactly at the junction of divided, one-way paving with a single, two-way paving. Partway around the nature trail the Humpback Creek trail takes off to the south and climbs up through the woods, roughly paralleling the course of the creek.

The trail breaks out of the trees at ¼ mile onto Forest Service road #22015, just east of a crossing of Humpback Creek. A powerline is ahead upslope, and the trail route follows the powerline service road, which goes steeply uphill from road #22015. There is a sign at this junction, but none 100 feet beyond, where the footpath leaves the service road and winds off through the bracken and salal towards wooded country again. From the clearing look back to a good view of Granite Mountain, across the Snoqualmie valley.

The way goes steadily along the course of Humpback Creek. At ¾ mile is the Milwaukee Railroad; the crossing is not at right angles, but jogs to the right about 25 feet. Then begins a series of steep switchbacks up the west side of Silver Peak, gaining 1200 feet in the next 1½ miles, and providing some nice views of Humpback Mountain from openings created by avalanches. The last mile contours to the lake at the 3600-foot level.

The east shore is National Forest, but the other three sides are private property. Half the shore is level and provides attractive places to camp; 500-foot cliffs opposite form an enclosure decorated with cascading waterfalls. Abiel Peak, 5365 feet high, stands on the south. Silver Peak, nearby to the east, is a favorite with climbers, who sometimes approach it from Annette Lake.

Round trip 6½ miles
Allow 5 hours
High point 3600 feet
Elevation gain 1600 feet
Best June through November
One day or backpack

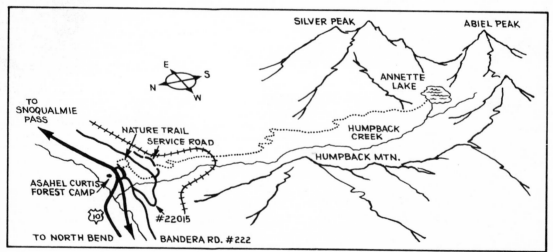

Annette Lake and Abiel Peak

5   GRANITE MOUNTAIN

A broad view from the summit ridge over peaks and lakes of the Snoqualmie Pass region. The high slopes are a rock garden of granite blocks and arid-land flowers.

Drive east on US 10 from North Bend about 17 miles to a small sign on the right, "Denny Creek". Turn left, then left again, on the westbound highway, drive ½ mile to a side road right to parking area and start of trail.

The first mile is along the excellent Pratt Lake Trail through heavy forest. At the junction with the Granite Mountain Trail a little brook provides water — from late summer on, the last reliable supply. The easy part is now over. The trail from here, up to the right, is long and steep, and in sunny weather, hot. (In summer, start early to beat the heat.) Forest continues for another half-mile; thereafter the trail ascends an open south-facing slope. Right in the middle of the hottest part there may be a stream still running from a snowfield on the summit, but don't count on it after July. The trail zig-zags and traverses to the summit ridge. For the best view one need not go all the way to the top; walk to the east end of the ridge and look out over all the Snoqualmie Pass peaks, and down to Denny Lake and Tuscohatchie Lakes, and southeast to Lake Keechelus.

The trail goes west along the summit ridge with meadows on the left and cirques on the right. On top is an operating lookout. The look-out tower and the junction with the Granite Mountain Trail are both on private property; the rest is Snoqualmie National Forest.

Round trip to lookout 9 miles
Allow 6 hours
High point 5629 feet
Elevation gain 3733 feet
Best early summer or fall
One day

Snoqualmie Pass from Granite Mountain viewpoint

6   PRATT LAKE

A long but easy hike, mostly in heavy forest, to a large lake set deep in subalpine trees. Close by is the boulder-strewn summit of 5099-foot Pratt Mountain.

Drive east on US 10 from North Bend about 17 miles to a small sign on the right, "Denny Creek". Turn left, then left again, on the westbound highway, drive ½ mile to a side road right to parking area and start of trail.

The trail gains 800 feet through deep forest in the first mile. Good opportunity for water and rest at 1 mile, where a side trail to Granite Mountain branches off uphill to the right and a brook crosses the main trail. At 3 miles is another good resting spot, the Lookout Shelter, built as a memorial to a Seattle Boy Scout killed in World War II. The shelter has had hard, thoughtless usage, but enough remains to moderate the force of wind and rain.

At 3½ miles is a short side trail left to Olallie Lake. Beyond here the dense forest gradually yields to more open growth as the trail circles the lake to ascend the Pratt Lake divide, highest point of the journey, and with a fine view of Mt. Rainier. Beyond a junction at 4 miles with a side trail left to Pratt Mountain and Mt. Defiance, the Pratt Lake Trail drops an abrupt mile down the north side of the divide, levels off about 200 feet above the lake, and contours along to the outlet at the north end, where there are good level campsites. Huge silver logs piled in confu-sion across the outlet provide a choice of accommodations for eating, resting, or carefree log-hopping.

Less than a half-mile farther along the trail is the less-frequented but very beautiful Lower Tuscohatchie Lake (large shelter here), highly recommended as an alternate objective.

Round trip 12 miles
Allow 8 hours
High point 4160 feet
Elevation gain 2264 feet
Best July through October
One day or backpack

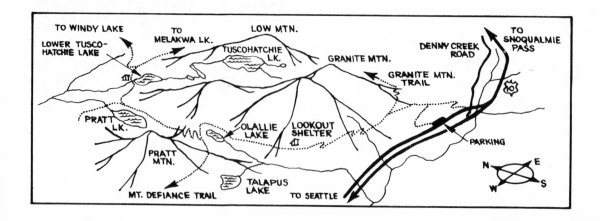

Fallen tree along the Pratt Lake Trail

7 MELAKWA LAKE

A gem of a lake beneath 6000-foot peaks. A huge boulder on the shore provides a perfect spot for admiring the scene.

Drive east on US 10 from North Bend about 17 miles to a small sign on the right, "Denny Creek". Turn left, then left again onto the west bound highway, drive ½ mile to a forest road right; follow it straight ahead about 3 miles. Pass the main entrance of Denny Creek Forest Camp, turn left on the next road, cross the Snoqualmie River, continue to the parking area and trail.

Trail #1014 ascends Denny Creek fairly gradually for 1½ miles to Keekwulee Falls, then switchbacks up a very steep rise. Care should be taken here; the way lies along the edge of a deep ravine. Above Snowshoe Falls, about 2½ miles, the trail again flattens out in the head of Denny Creek basin. From here on and including the lake is an entire section (one square mile) of private property. The trail switchbacks up to Hemlock Pass and descends—but not much—into forests adjoining Melakwa Lake on the west.

Here, near the outlet, is the observation platform. The water is clear and still, remnants of snow on the opposite cliffs are startling white, steep peaks form a wall all around the east shore. Good campsites in trees on the west and on a high promontory at the north.

The energetic and speedy hiker can make a 16-mile trip by continuing to Tuscohatchie Lake, Pratt Lake, Olallie Lake, and thence back to US 10, 3½ miles from the parking area.

Another trip popular with travelers of some off-trail experience crosses Melakwa Pass, drops to Iceberg Lake, and continues on to Snow Lake and from there to the highway at Snoqualmie Pass.

Round trip 8 miles
Allow 6 hours
High point 4500 feet
Elevation gain 2180 feet
Best July 15 to October 15
One day or backpack

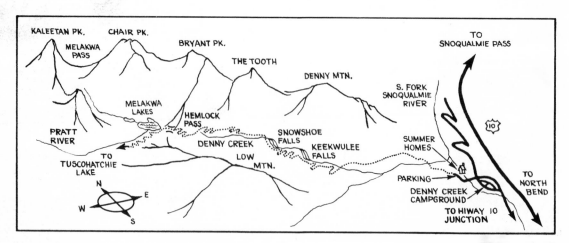

Keekwulee Falls on Denny Creek

8   SNOW LAKE

The Cascade Crest Trail north from Snoqualmie Pass leads to this large lake with rugged peaks on one side and the great gulf of the Middle Fork of the Snoqualmie on the other.

Drive on US 10 to Snoqualmie Pass; park on turnout road across highway from the summit ski area. A large wooden sign-map is prominent; here begins the trail.

First walking is through old forest on wide smooth trail. Confusion may occur if signs are missing at a road which has been cut through the trail; foot travelers should jog to the right up the road about 100 feet; the footpath leads off again on the far side of the road. At ½ mile is a junction with trails left and right along Commonwealth Creek, just beyond which the Snow Lake trail crosses the creek, climbs an embankment and opens onto a private ski hill. To regain the route where it continues beyond this clearing, contour, making a slight gain in elevation. Thereafter the trail follows Source Creek, some distance above the stream, passing through a new ski cabin subdivision, and ascends gradually for 4 miles to curve around the basin wall above Source Lake, a tiny pond in a cirque at the eastern base of 6000-foot Chair Peak. In the next ½ mile the trail gains 500 feet in elevation, very steeply, to the ridge separating Snow Lake from Source Lake, and Middle Fork drainage from the South Fork. A fine view from here.

The trail descends sharply, on private prop-erty, to mile-long Snow Lake, surrounded in season by acres of blueberries. Many good campsites; some of the best are on private property on the northeast shore near the cascading outlet, overlooking the Middle Fork valley.

Hikers seeking more seclusion may continue past Snow Lake approximately 1½ miles to little Gem Lake, whose admirers praise it enthusiastically. Still another 1½ miles distant is Wildcat Lake. This additional travel is entirely on private property, except for Wildcat Lake itself.

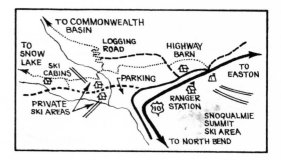

Round trip 11 miles
Allow 7 hours
High point 4400 feet
Elevation gain 1800 feet
Best July through October
One day or backpack

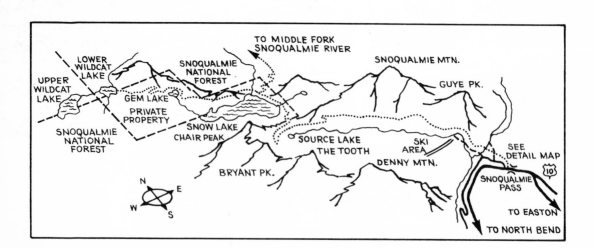

Trail to Snow Lake with Guye Peak in the distance

The last stand of Snoqualmie Pass wilderness—threatened but still intact. Subalpine forests, a clear cool stream, and an easy trail to meadows and views. Good for a leisurely afternoon with little children, a busy day for climbers, a peaceful overnight camp, or variations.

Drive on U.S. 10 to Snoqualmie Pass. Park on turnout road north of highway, directly opposite the summit ski area. Trail begins at the large Forest Service trail directory sign.

The first ¼ mile is flat, beside meadow-marshes due to be wiped out eventually by a limited-access freeway. Then comes a logging road—jog right about 100 feet to find the trail continuation, watching for Cascade Crest Trail signs. At ½ mile is a junction; Snow Lake trail goes ahead, Commonwealth Basin right. The next ½ mile climbs bleak logging shambles and roads; if signs are missing, look for boot tracks. At the lip of the basin the path enters unmolested (as yet) forest; pause here to scan the area of super-development behind and below, the quintessence of multiple-use.

Just into the trees, note a collapsed cabin across the creek; take a moment off-trail to enjoy rockslabs and pools of the waterfall. The trail follows Commonwealth Creek, several times crossing the stream or its branches, passing many popular campsites. Guye Peak is on the left and Kendall on the right. As the grade lessens somewhat in the upper basin, Snoqualmie Moun-tain, Lundin Peak, and unmistakably red Red Mountain come into sight. Now there is a rather stern passage, up and up short switchbacks along the spine of a spur ridge from Red, but the sky grows with every step and at the top is a boulder-strewn cirque lakelet with snow water and heather-bed camps.

From Red Pond the trail goes up some more, traversing talus and rock buttresses to the "pass" between Red and Lundin—except this is not the trail pass, which is a bit to the west on the crest. Admire the vast valley of the Middle Fork of the Snoqualmie River, the tower of Mt. Thompson, horizons east and north with Cascades near and distant, and south over Snoqualmie Pass to Rainier. To gain an easy peak with broader views, follow a boot-beaten track up heather nooks and blueberry slopes to a little summit next to Lundin. See the mountain climbers in action.

Round trip to pass 7 miles
Allow 5 hours
High point 5360 feet
Elevation gain 2360 feet
Best July 15 to October 15
One day or backpack

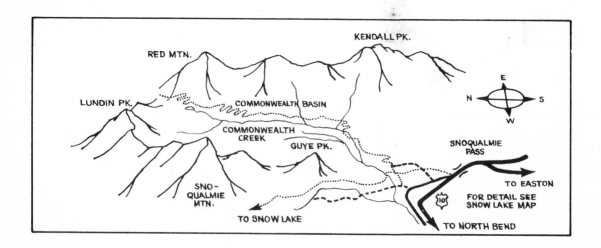

Red Mountain from Commonwealth Basin

10 SNOQUALMIE LAKE

A beautiful, big subalpine lake edged by hillsides of Alaska cedar and mountain hemlock, with harsh cliffs protruding.

Drive on US 10 to 4 miles east of North Bend. (US 10 is a divided highway here. If approaching from the east, one is already in the correct lane. If approaching from the west, drive about 4½ miles east from North Bend to a Washington State Patrol weighing station, maneuver onto the west-bound lane, and drive ½ mile back toward North Bend.) Turn right on Edgewick Road, bear left ½ mile to an intersection, turn right and follow the course of the Middle Fork Snoqualmie River on Forest Service Road #2445. (At 1½ miles keep right, at 2¾ miles go straight ahead, at 3¼ miles keep left.) About 15 miles, just across the Taylor River, keep left and follow #2445 along the Taylor River to road-end, where trail begins. Park leaving space for other cars to turn around.

The grade is gentle at first, following closely beside the Taylor River. At ½ mile is a junction with a trail, right, to Nordrum Lake. From this point the Snoqualmie Lake trail climbs for 2 miles with long switchbacks, passing near the roar of mighty Nordrum Falls. As elevation is gained, the hemlock and white fir forest changes gradually to cedar. The trail finally curves southward for a last ½ mile, still following the stream, and reaches the lake shore near a great promontory. Good locations for camping or lunching abound, each with an outlook over this isolated haven of serene waters and mountainous borders.

The trail winds around the north side of Snoqualmie Lake, then continues past Deer and Bear Lakes to ascend the low divide between the Taylor River and Miller River drainages, 2½ miles from Snoqualmie Lake. A fine view from this ridge, overlooking Lake Dorothy and the Miller River valley north and 6670-foot Big Snow Mountain to the southeast. One can descend by trail to Lake Dorothy and the Miller River Road, leading to US 2.

Round trip 6 miles
Allow 4 hours
High point 3225 feet
Elevation gain 1225 feet
Best July 15 to October 15
One day or backpack

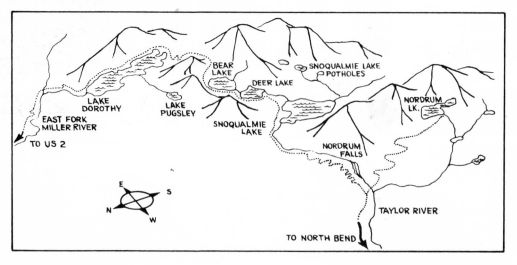

Snoqualmie Lake

11   DUTCH MILLER GAP

Rugged mountains rise above the forest and flank both sides of the narrow gap named for an early prospector. An exceptionally scenic trip along the Cascade Crest Trail following the Middle Fork Snoqualmie River to its source.

Drive on US 10 to 4 miles east of North Bend. (US 10 is a divided highway here. If approaching from the east, one is already in the correct lane. If approaching from the west, drive about 4½ miles east from North Bend to a Washington State Patrol weighing station, maneuver onto the west-bound lane, and drive ½ mile back toward North Bend.) Turn right on Edgewick Road, bear left ½ mile to an intersection, turn right and follow the course of the Middle Fork Snoqualmie River on Forest Service road #2445. (At 1½ miles keep right, at 2¾ miles go straight ahead, at 3¼ miles keep left.) About 15 miles, just across Taylor River, turn right onto road #241 and continue past Goldmeyer Hot Springs spur to the end of the road, where a private mining claim has been logged. Park well to the side of road, leaving room for others to pass.

Somewhere amid the muck and slash of timber-cutting is the beginning of the trail, but the marking signs may be missing, and the tangle of bulldozer tracks is bewildering. The way follows the course of the river in a northeasterly direction as best it can until beyond Hardscrabble Creek. The rest is easy.

The scenery is absolutely splendid: a wild tumbling river on one side, screened by the jungle-like growth of Western Washington forest, and towering over all, steep, sharp peaks.

Several miles above Hardscrabble the trail climbs a short, steep step in the valley and at the top opens out into subalpine country with heather, flowers, and broad views. Around 6 miles a large stream is crossed by bridge. (Fording may be required if the bridge is down.) A short distance farther one may notice remnants of Dutch Miller's cabin in a small clearing. Around 6½ miles, where the trail crosses the river (here no more than a creek), an obscure side trail, left, leads to La Bohn Gap, with a half-dozen rock-basin ponds, interesting old mine works, and a striking view down to Necklace Valley. The main trail continues to Dutch Miller Gap, 7 miles from the start, and the prototype of Japanese gardens: a small meadowland cut with tiny waterfalls and dark pools, trimmed with rocks and dwarf trees.

The favored places for camping are at the Gap. Other good campsites are available at convenient intervals all along the trail.

Round trip 14 miles
Allow 2 days
High point 5000 feet
Elevation gain 2500 feet
Best July through September
Backpack

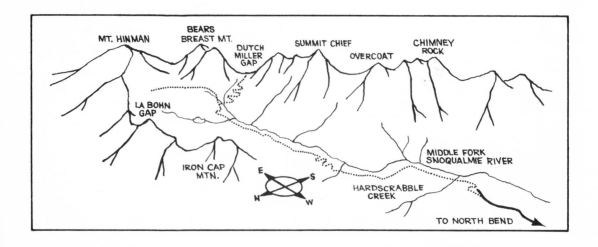

Trail to Dutch Miller Gap

12   LAKE LILLIAN

Short and not difficult hike to meadows and high lakes, with a side trip to a nearby summit and good views of the Snoqualmie Pass region.

Drive on US 10 east from Snoqualmie Pass about 6 miles and turn left at Rocky Run Forest Camp, then drive on logging road #2216. After about 1½ miles this road enters a section of privately owned logging land and becomes a maze of branching spurs, poorly signed. An approximate description of the route is: Go four hairpin turns, take left fork. Go one hairpin turn, through a clearing, then just upon entering the timber again, turn right. Take next fork left up a steep spur to end. The last mile of the logging road is in extremely poor condition; one might be happier hiking rather than driving it. Trail starts at very topmost end, identified by blazes and inconspicuous sign.

Both logging road and trail are within the official boundaries of Wenatchee National Forest, but half their distance is over privately owned property where logging is constantly changing the terrain. The trail itself is not recognized by the Forest Service.

The blazed trail goes straight to the ridge where it intersects an old trail. (This junction is very easy to miss on the way down, so examine it carefully.) Once on the ridge, the trail is easy to follow. After about a mile a side trail, right, goes to Margaret Lake. Shortly past this junction the trail leaves the ridge to contour around the

mountain, and from here one can reach the summit by following any of numerous spur tracks up to a false summit. The view is good, but to reach the real summit follow the ridge up and down for another ¼ mile. A remarkable view of Snoqualmie Pass peaks and Lake Keechelus west and small lakes east.

The main trail contours around the north side of the mountain, then drops down an open ridge of alpine meadows and few trees to Twin Lakes. The trail from here to Lake Lillian is rough and fairly steep, with some mud and brush. Rampart Ridge is a short and easy stroll from the meadow-surrounded lake and gives an even better view than that from Margaret. A room-sized cave in the heights just above the lake, quite easy to find, is another feature of interest. Good campsites at both Twin Lakes and Lake Lillian.

Round trip to Lillian 6 miles
Allow 4 hours
High point 5520 feet
Elevation gain to Margaret 960 feet, plus 840 feet to Lillian
Best June through September
One day or backpack

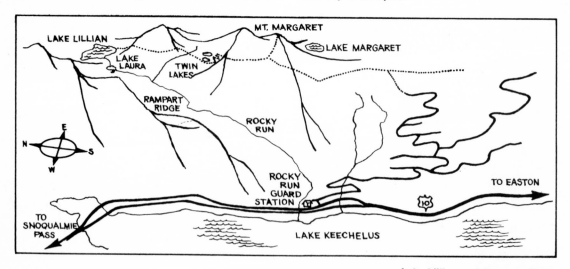

Lake Lillian and Rampart Ridge

13   RAMPART RIDGE

A hiker was once heard to say, arriving at Rampart Lakes, "If this isn't Heaven, when my time comes I'll refuse to go."

Drive on US 10 east from Snoqualmie Pass 10½ miles. Turn left on road to Lake Kachess; follow signs to Box Canyon road. At 5 miles from US 10 turn left beyond Lake Kachess Guard Station on road #2214. Go 4 miles, crossing Box Canyon Creek, to a fork. Turn left on road signed "Rachel Lake trail." In .3 mile, just this side of bridge over North Fork Canyon Creek, park on shoulder. Trail #1313, signed, starts to right.

The first mile is moderately but steadily up-hill; stop for a cold drink and to examine water-sculptured, pot-holed slabs and also mossy slabs. The next 1½ miles are pretty level, mostly near the creek, with several detours around avalanche-downed trees. Passages through head-high greenery, where one may have to foot-probe for the tread early in the season, before traffic beats the bushes down. Many mud-holes. In short, trail maintenance is slight—but no matter, it keeps the scooters out. Views to Hibox above on the right. At about 2½ miles the trail runs into the valley headwall and quits fooling around, climbing 1400 feet in a mile, with few switchbacks. That's steep. However, at 3½ miles 4700-foot Rachel Lake makes the sweat worthwhile. Campsites everywhere. Explore lakeside tracks, especially left, where a narrow channel connects to a secluded and unexpected "extra" lake.

The official trail, such as it is, ends at Rachel. The trip should not. Turn right at lakeshore on unofficial but easy path, curve around the cirque, climbing into open slopes with looks down to sparkling Rachel and out Box Canyon Creek to the dangerous encroachments of logging. Gain 500 feet in ½ mile to a broad 5200-foot saddle and an unmarked trail fork between Rampart and Alta. Turn right a mile to Lila Lake and/or a stroll to the summit of 6240-foot Alta. Or turn left for a scant up-and-down mile to 5100-foot Rampart Lakes.

The photograph suggests what to expect: rock-set tarns of various sizes and depths, with islands that make swimming almost mandatory. Wander through meadows, around buttresses, beside ponds and waterfalls, interesting rocks—basalts, conglomerates, mineralized red masses—into nooks and over knolls, to the crest of Rampart Ridge. Views into Gold Creek, west to Snoqualmie Pass peaks, east to Mt. Stuart, south to Rainier, north to Three Queens, Chimney Rock.

Round trip 10 miles
Allow 8 hours
High point 5200 feet
Elevation gain 2400 feet
Best June through October
One day or backpack

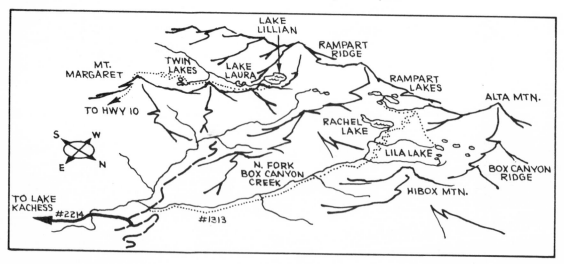

Air view of lakes on Rampart Ridge

14   WALLACE FALLS

Prominent waterfall, now within a new but as yet undeveloped state park, visible to the north of US 2 as one approaches Goldbar from the west. Obviously surrounded by forests for miles on all sides, from a distance the torrent appears mysterious and unattainable, yet can be reached by a well-traveled path.

Drive east on US 2 to just inside the town of Goldbar. Turn left (north) on the western-most through street (Standard Station on corner). Cross a bridge, turn right. At "Y" intersection go left. Cross another bridge and park nearby on shoulder. The main road curves right and ends at Camp Huston. A dirt road disappears to the left off the curve. About 25 feet up this dirt road is an almost hidden abandoned road, to the right, along which the hike begins, going up through the woods behind Camp Huston.

At ¼ mile the old road reaches a power line and crosses diagonally under. On the far side a trail continues through a narrow opening between the bushes, going along a wide, man-made causeway, smoothly ascending and well-drained. However, the narrow trail up the middle of the causeway is crowded with brush, wet going in rainy weather.

The trail switchbacks sharply right at 1 mile. In another mile it reaches a wide place, the junction of several old roads. Straight ahead across the clearing goes the path, on an old railroad grade, parts of which still show ballast and the striations

of old railroad ties. Mt. Stickney rises directly ahead, and seems to be the destination. However, the trail turns aside at 2½ miles, at a well-used campsite in a small clearing. An inconspicuous trail to the right winds in and out among rocks and tree roots down a narrow ridge to the noisy North Fork of the Wallace River and a sturdy rustic bridge.

The beginner may find the next 10 minutes of steep hillside quite exhausting. Slow, careful going is required. The trail levels off through beautiful open forests, and now a new sound fills the air — the roar of Wallace Falls. A last short climb leads to a viewpoint perched at one side of the falls on precipitous slopes marked off with a rope fence. Most hikers are content to eat lunch here and then return. Others may wish to climb another 160 feet to the top of the falls, where there is a fine picnic spot beside the stream and interesting exploring. All this area near the falls is dangerous to the unwary, with steep soft slopes hidden by woods and underbrush, and slippery rocks above wild waters.

Round trip 6 miles
Allow 4½ hours
High point 1120 feet
Elevation gain 880 feet
Best early spring or in fall
One day

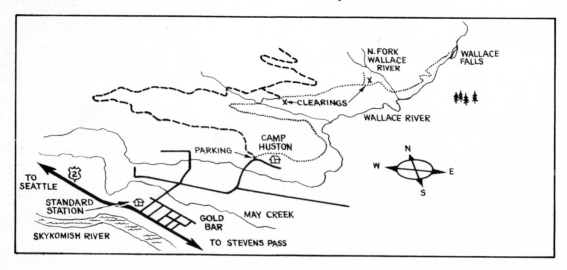

Wallace Falls

15   LAKE SERENE

A ruggedly beautiful lake tucked in a pocket beneath the 3000-foot east wall of Mt. Index; getting there is more a scramble than a walk, but well worth the struggle—which is short.

Drive east on US 2 beyond Goldbar some 5 miles. Watch for "Swanson's Cabins" sign, then slow down and turn right onto a dirt road just before a bridge over the Skykomish River. Turn right at the second turnoff, go approximately 1.4 miles to a fork, where small signs warn against going farther. Do not block either fork; space for two or three cars off the road.

Hikers have the established legal right to pass through this property. Begin by walking along the right fork of the road, passing through or around the gate at the entrance to the Honeymoon Mine. From the truck-loading structure, the trail can be located in bushy growth to the left, bearing southeast and uphill. There is no sign.

This trail is not for beginners. It is hard to find and when found isn't much: narrow, brushy, rocky, and often requiring hands as well as feet. However, tough as the going is, the total distance to the lake is less than a mile. After about 300 feet distance, if on the right trail, one comes to an opening with a view of the Skykomish valley, surrounding mountains, and Heybrook Lookout across the river. Farther along is a decrepit bridge, wobbly at best, now almost useless. A bypass is being tramped around it.

Once safely over, clamber straightforwardly up the hillside on step-like projections of tree roots to an old miners' cabin. A side trip around the back of this relic is worthwhile for a memorable view of Bridal Veil Falls; also as the last chance for drinking water—there is none before the lake.

From the front porch of the cabin the trail plunges into cool, shady forest a few hundred feet to an old mine shaft, around a small cliff beyond the shaft, then up, straight up—over tree roots and boulders, through mud, but always up, not flattening out until within a few steps of the lake. A short stroll around the shore to the right is a huge rounded rock ideal for lunching or sunning or examining the cliffs of Index. Around to the left at the spillway is a fine view north across the valley. Abrupt cliffs on this side beyond the outlet make circling the lake extremely hazardous. Campsites are available but rather grubby because of over-use.

Late spring is a particularly attractive time for this walk: the trail is often free of snow in early or middle May while the lake is still frozen solid and partly covered by a monster avalanche cone from the cliffs of Index.

Round trip 2 miles
Allow 5 hours
High point 2500 feet
Elevation gain 1500 feet
Best June through November
One day or backpack

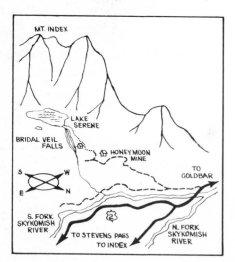

Lake Serene and Mount Index

16   HEYBROOK LOOKOUT

Easy walk along a woods road to a fine view of valley and peaks. Especially attractive as an early-spring or early-winter trip; because of the low elevation, the snow comes late and doesn't stay long, and in open winters hardly comes at all. Also good as a rainy-weather hike, since no wet brush crowds the way.

Drive on US 2 east from Index junction about 3 miles to several small houses on the right. Two wooden gates on the left side of the road bar crossings over the railroad. Park off the highway, **not** in front of the gates or the houses. Walk around a gate, cross the railroad, and proceed up the gravel road which leads to the left on the far side of the tracks.

The road goes uphill promptly, passing a tiny stream (right) which has been carefully cleared and rocked-in; a good canteen-filling spot. The way follows a nearby creek half a mile or more to the Bonneville power line, jogs left along it a few hundred feet, then turns right and uphill again, crossing the creek and entering briefly onto private property, then recrossing the creek. Hikers cross private property at three places during this trip, but most of the land is within Snoqualmie National Forest.

From here the road extends along the middle of the ridge in a northwesterly direction all the way to the lookout, mounting gradually almost to the highest point of the ridge, then slipping onto the south side to the lookout clearing. The 73-foot prefabricated tower is of recent construction and interesting for this fact alone, since a really modern lookout building is a curiosity. Excellent views of Index, Baring, and other peaks, and of Bridal Veil Falls across the Skykomish valley.

Round trip 8 miles
Allow 4 hours
High point 1701 feet
Elevation gain 980 feet
Best April through November
One day

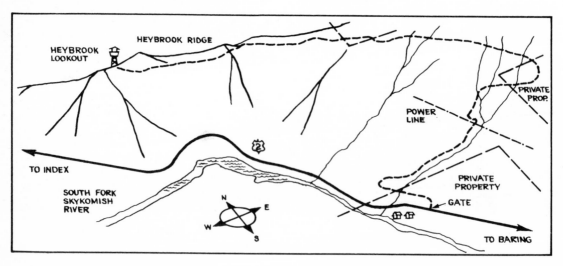

Mount Index and Mount Persis from Heybrook Lookout

17   LAKE BLANCA

A large blue-green lake sitting in a deep cirque framed by Columbia, Monte Cristo, and Kyes Peaks, fed by meltwater from ice in the trough above.

Drive on US 2 to Index junction, turn left along the North Fork of the Skykomish River to Garland Mineral Springs, 5 miles beyond Troublesome Creek Campground. Take dirt road left for 2 miles to sign marking Lake Blanca Trail. Park at side of road.

The trail starts uphill right away and switchbacks steeply through pleasant forest. After a couple of miles Glacier Peak is framed through openings in the trees. At 3 miles is the top of the ridge, and the highest elevation of the trip. The trail passes through trees and meadows along the ridge to a shallow pond. The comfortable campsites here may tempt those who have found the 2900-foot climb sufficient for the day. However, Lake Blanca is only another easy mile away, and worth the added effort.

From here the trail goes downhill, for Lake Blanca lies in the canyon west of the ridge. The trail is narrow and may be muddy in spots. Partway down, the lake can be glimpsed as a light bluish-green patch through the trees.

After more than 500 feet of descent, the trail comes to the shore near the outlet, and the blue-green is seen to be real. And cold. Columbia Glacier, in the trough above the inlet, feeds the ¾-mile-wide lake with icy waterfalls. Good camp-sites where the trail meets the lake and also along the left shore. A side trail leads to the nearby outlet stream rumbling down a narrow gorge on its way to Troublesome Creek. Advanced hikers can explore the north end of the lake and continue clear up to the glacier; those with proper alpine gear and experience can climb over the col and descend into Glacier Basin, above Monte Cristo.

Round trip 8½ miles
Allow 6-8 hours
High point 4600 feet
Elevation gain 2900 feet, descent 500 feet
Best July through October
One day or backpack

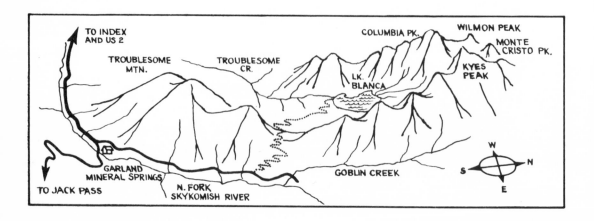

Air view of Lake Blanca and Kyes Peak

18   BARCLAY LAKE

Though the trail gains elevation slowly and steadily, the hiker may have the sensation of going down, down, down into the earth. The valley which holds him grows ever narrower, the steep mountain masses loom ever closer and higher, until at journey's end he rests in what seems like a tiny deep room, one wall of which is all rock and 3000 feet high.

Drive on US 2 east 5.7 miles beyond Index junction. Turn left on road marked by arrow pointing to Baring. Cross railroad tracks, go straight ahead .7 mile, part of the way under the power line, to a sign at the start of the trail. Plentiful parking space at roadside.

The trail quickly leaves the power line and plunges into deep forest, rising very gradually to pass around the steepest parts of the west ridge of Mt. Baring. This is mostly National Forest land, but from 1½ to 3 miles the trail passes through private property. The splendid trees are marked for logging, and the lovely forest may now be gone. If logging is not underway, the sounds of rushing water can be heard, faintly, then louder, until at 2 miles the white rapids of Barclay Creek can be seen. About 3 miles, the trail for the second time nears the tumbling stream close enough so that water can be reached; good campsite here. At another good campsite, ½ mile farther on, the creek forms clear pools of deep, quiet water. About 4 miles, the trail crosses the creek on 50-foot logs felled by the Forest Service

and fashioned into simple footbridges, flattened on top, and reassuringly provided with handrails of heavy wire. At the far end of the footlogs is a campsite under the trees, with a thrilling view of Baring's north wall. But only one more mile of hiking leads to Barclay Lake, where one can camp—or rest—beside a quiet lake surrounded by mountains. Two miles beyond Barclay Lake— and steeply above—is Eagle Lake, with an impressive cross-valley look at Baring's cliff, and with more view easily reached by scrambling up ridges.

The trail is well-maintained but in wet seasons has many stretches of deep, black mud and difficult walking.

Round trip 10 miles
Allow 7 hours
High point 2950 feet
Elevation gain 2000 feet
Best April to November 15
One day or backpack

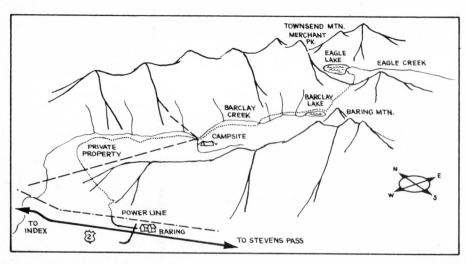

Barclay Lake and Mount Baring

19 EVERGREEN MOUNTAIN

Open woods most of the way permit good views at higher points. Alpine meadows and flowers along the summit ridge, and an operating fire lookout on top.

Drive on US 2 to the first road to the left east of Skykomish, the Beckler River Road. Go 7 miles on this road to Rapid River, turn right, then take left fork approximately 2 miles to sign, "Evergreen Mountain", at junction with old logging road left. Park on nearby shoulder. (Brave drivers with sturdy vehicles can shorten the walk by negotiating about 1 mile of the extremely rocky old logging road. Pass the second hairpin turn, then in about 400 feet watch for space to turn around. Park in the roadway, facing downhill.)

A short stretch near the beginning is over privately owned land, otherwise the entire hike is in Snoqualmie National Forest. From Rapid River Road the trail goes 2 miles along the disintegrating logging road, on cut-over tangled hillsides unprotected from sun or wind, crowded by brush, and roughed up by slides. It is refreshing, therefore, to pause just before the trail slips into the woods and look south down the Beckler River Valley.

Continuing above this viewpoint the trail follows the winding ridge crest. The trees are large and the undergrowth scant, allowing views into the forests on both sides. High on the mountain, note trees extending out from the hillside nearly horizontally for a foot or so before they begin to grow vertically. The young trees in wintertime have bent under the weight of snow with immediately resulting changes in the growth pattern of cells on their earthward sides. As maturity increases the trees become solid enough to withstand snow pressure, yet they retain permanently the curve of a more tender age.

There are only two reliable sources of water along the way. One is a little more than a mile from the Rapid River Road, where the old logging road has been thoroughly washed out by a vigorous stream. The other is about ½ mile from the summit where a marker indicates a side trail right ½ mile to a spring. Beyond this junction the trail breaks out of trees into meadows and the lookout tower comes into view. Broad panoramas in all directions, climaxed on the north by Glacier Peak. During fire season there may be an opportunity for a visit with a Forest Service lookout.

Round trip 12 miles
Allow 8 hours
High point 5585 feet
Elevation gain 3585 feet
Best July through October
One day

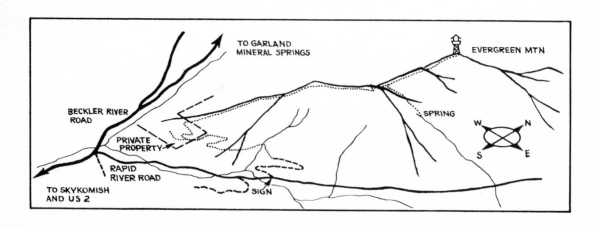

North towards Kyes Peak after an early fall snowstorm on Evergreen Mountain

An exceptional group of lakes, part of the proposed Alpine Lakes Wilderness where ice was once as plentiful as it still is a bit farther north in the Cascades, and in retreating has left lakes almost beyond number. A full baker's dozen form the headwaters of the West Fork of the Foss River, and on this trip the hiker can visit six conveniently by trail, beginning with Trout Lake, a short 1½ miles from the road, continuing to Malachite, Copper, Little Heart, Big Heart, and Angeline Lakes.

Drive east on US 2 from Skykomish about 1½ miles; turn right onto the Foss River road and drive approximately 7 miles to the end of the road, where trail begins.

The trail winds through shadowy forest and lush undergrowth. Lucid water flows gently in quiet pools apart from the main stream. Pause to admire a huge cedar leaning over the trail, and (at 1 mile) a grand old tree, almost 10 feet in diameter, bearing the marks of much buffeting. The last ½ mile to Trout Lake gains 400 feet up an ever-narrowing valley walled by irregular cliffs softened with patches of bush and fern, brightened by slim watercourses splashing down from lingering pockets of snow. At Trout Lake (1½ miles) the trail enters private property, which extends all along the west shore. A cool hemlock forest provides many fine campsites.

The trail continues steeply up slopes to the west of Trout Lake, once more in the National Forest, detouring around the 500-foot cascade which pours from Copper Lake. At 3½ miles a side trail right climbs to lonely Malachite Lake, fenced by a corral of talus, and in another cirque at 4 miles is Copper Lake, lying at 4000 feet, twice as high as Trout Lake. These lake shores have a character approaching alpine quality; hillsides are rocky and open, vegetation is comparatively thin, and ridge tops are close. They are good turnaround points for a one day hike.

The trail leads from Copper Lake over a low ridge to Little Heart Lake at 6 miles, then over a higher ridge (5000 feet) to end, at 8 miles, at Big Heart Lake, where there is a shelter cabin. Lake Angeline can be reached without difficulty by a way trail contouring east 1 mile from the outlet of Big Heart Lake. The more ambitious can travel cross-country to still other lakes nearby.

Round trip to Little Heart Lake 12 miles
Allow 11 hours
High point 5000 feet
Elevation gain 3500 feet
Best July through October
One day or backpack

Trail past Trout Lake

Copper Lake

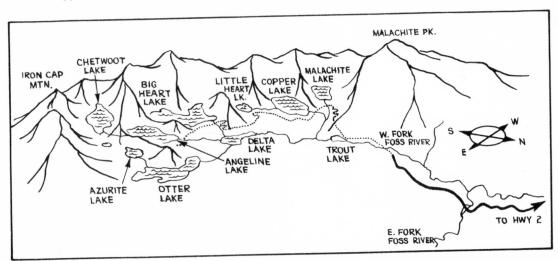

A rockbound lake reached through the heavy, moist forests west of Stevens Pass on an uncomplicated trail. Ramble to Glacier Lake, Surprise Gap, and—for view—the summit of Surprise Mountain.

Drive east on US 2 to sign, "Scenic"; don't turn. Cross a bridge over the Great Northern Railroad tracks and **immediately** at end of bridge turn right on dirt road. At road fork and sign, "Surprise Lake", turn left. Somewhat before a large Forest Service sign ("Cascade Crest Trail" and "Surprise Lake") an obvious parking area is suitable for several cars to get off the roadway.

The trail is somewhat brushy at first, rocky in places, and quite muddy. Posted notices state that it is not recommended for horses, but riders use it anyway, deepening the mud until it is a nuisance, especially for hiking parties with small children.

About 1 mile Surprise Creek is crossed on a footlog. The trees are closely spaced and there is little to see except the tops of a few peaks and (in season) the flourishing mushrooms on the forest floor. At one point the woods open enough for a view back down the valley and ahead to Surprise Mountain. At 4 miles, when the lake is just visible, a clearing makes a good camping place. Here the trail joins the Cascade Crest Trail.

Hikers up for the day usually explore around the lake, eat, snooze, then return downtrail. Those with more time can travel the Crest Trail to

Glacier Lake at 5 miles, and ½ mile farther to a leanto shelter in a small flat meadow southeast of the lake. (Campsites at both.) The Crest Trail then climbs through a granite basin to Surprise Gap at 6½ miles, 1000 feet higher than Glacier Lake, over steep, rocky switchbacks where hazardous snow patches usually remain until mid-July.

The 6300-foot summit of Surprise Mountain, 7½ miles, provides a panorama of the Cascades from the glaciers of Mount Daniel on the south to those of Glacier Peak on the north.

Round trip 8 miles
Allow 6 hours
High point 4600 feet
Elevation gain 2500 feet
Best June through October
One day or backpack

Junior Mountaineers cleaning up Surprise Lake

Mount Daniel from Surprise Gap

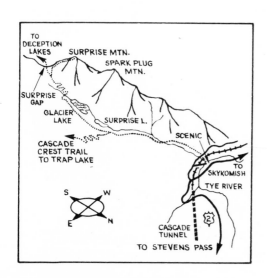

22   LAKE JOSEPHINE

An ideal first backpack trip. Mossy forests, slides of gray rock, a tiny storybook lake, valley views, miniature meadows laced with narrow streams, and a large blue oval lake deep in a rocky basin: a rich sampler of what makes Cascade hiking great.

Drive to Stevens Pass on US 2; park in designated area. Trail begins on south side of highway: it is marked, but poorly. Beyond the main ski lodge 200 feet, head uphill along the east edge of a small creek, past water reservoir on right.

The trail is well-maintained and quite good except for several patches of deep, black mud which must be crossed on slippery logs or elaborately bypassed.

Once above the ski slopes the path enters deep forest, cool and dim on a hot day, and progresses steadily upward, passing some rockslides as the hillside steepens and the trees thin out. Tracks of the Great Northern Railroad run through the Cascade Tunnel deep in the mountain beneath. The trail zig-zags up the last incline to the top of the Cascade divide at 1 mile, only to wind down again on the opposite side to the Bonneville Power Administration service road.

The direction signs at this point are confusing, and in a fog are impossible to see. Go left down the road about ½ mile; the road makes a turn to the right, and then another one to the left, at a tower. Do not make this left turn, but continue in an almost straight line out into the cutover area, watching for little rock cairns on stumps left by hikers to aid humanity. Head for a white diamond, the Pacific Crest Trail System marker, on a tree at the edge of the clearing.

At 2½ miles the headwaters of Mill Creek form in a bend of the divide where small meadows are partitioned by strips and hillocks of forest, and hikers easily spring over the infant streams. (The ubiquitous mud is unfortunately less avoidable.) The trailway next traverses an open rockslide from which one can see the length of Mill Creek valley and away across Nason Creek to distinguish the outline of Rock Mountain Lookout.

At 3 miles is a good campsite at picturesque Lake Susan Jane, then uphill another ½ mile to a junction with the Icicle Creek trail, left. For almost a mile the Icicle Creek trail descends the rim of the huge rock basin of Lake Josephine, with glimpses of blue water through the trees. At lake level, 4½ miles, near the outlet, are several excellent campsites.

Return the same route, or continue along the Cascade Crest Trail to Hope Lake, 3½ miles from the Icicle Creek trail junction, and then go down Tunnel Creek trail 2½ miles to US 2 near Scenic, 5 miles or so west of Stevens summit.

Round trip 9 miles
Allow 7 hours
High point 5500 feet
Elevation gain 1433 feet
Best July 15 through September
One day or backpack

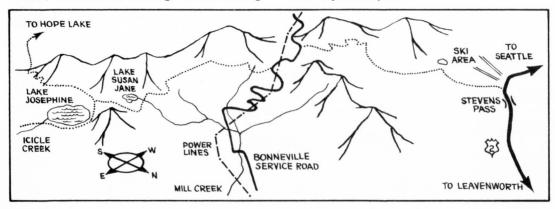

Cascade Crest Trail to Lake Josephine

23 LAKE VALHALLA

The Cascade Crest Trail north from Stevens Pass follows the divide which separates Columbia River waters from those which flow into Puget Sound. The first alpine lake the traveler reaches is Lake Valhalla, in a rocky basin almost at the divide summit, draining into Nason Creek, the Wenatchee River, and the Columbia. A splendid feature of the trip is that—being on the Crest Trail—motorized vehicles do not violate the path.

Drive to Stevens Pass on US 2. Park at the east end of the summit parking area. Signs indicating Cascade Crest Trail are behind the service buildings.

The way leads north following the old Great Northern Railroad right-of-way used before the original Cascade Tunnel was opened early in the century. Needless to say, the grade is very easy for the foot-traveler. Far below, Stevens Creek parallels the route, and cars and trucks move along the highway. At 1½ miles the trail swings west around the toe of the ridge, leaving Stevens Creek where it and Valhalla Creek join to become Nason Creek. A side trail leads east from here to the old Cascade Tunnel ½ mile away.

The trail to the lake drops down to cross a small stream, then climbs another ridge. At 3½ miles it curves around the inside of a basin, keeping somewhat below the crest, ascends gradually to an elevation of over 5000 feet, and then ducks down to the rocky west shore of the lake. On the far shore rise the high cliffs of Lichtenberg

Mountain. The lake is popular with backpackers; there are several good campsites among the trees.

Lake Valhalla can also be reached from the Smith Brook Trail, which involves a shorter hiking distance and less time. Drive east from Stevens Pass on US 2 about 3½ miles and take the Smith Brook road, Forest Service #2714, left about 1½ miles to its end. The trail ascends Smith Brook about 1½ miles, there intersecting the Cascade Crest Trail which leads right to Lake Janus and left to Lake Valhalla, about 2 miles south.

Round trip 11 miles
Allow 6 hours
High point 5100 feet
Elevation gain 1039 feet
Best July 15 to October 15
One day or backpack

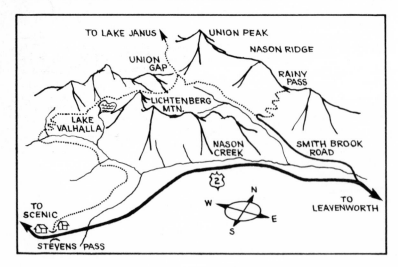

Lake Valhalla from Lichtenberg Pass

24   ALPINE LOOKOUT

Views of Lake Wenatchee, Nason Creek valley, and the Chiwaukum Mountains from a fire lookout atop wonderfully scenic Nason Ridge, above the Stevens Pass highway.

Drive on US 2 east from Stevens Pass past Merritt 3 miles to an emergency airfield on the right, recognizable by the red and white pylons. Take next left on Butcher Creek road #2717, marked (subsequent to publication of this book) with Forest Service sign, "Alpine Lookout—Home of the Mountain Goats." Avoiding spur roads (approximately 1½ miles, turn right; approximately 2½ miles, turn sharp left), drive almost to the end of the road; trail starts at sign.

The well-maintained trail climbs Round Mountain by an easy grade to the crest of Nason Ridge, then follows the ridge west to the lookout, about 4 miles. Views in both directions: north over Lake Wenatchee and the wide White River valley and south across the Stevens Pass highway to the Chiwaukum Mountains and McCue Ridge.

For an interesting return, continue west from Alpine Lookout, still along the crest of Nason Ridge, dipping and rising with it for 4 miles to a trail junction just above Merritt Lake. Ahead the Nason Ridge trail goes on and on some 13 miles more, past Rock Mountain Lookout, the entire length of Nason Ridge. Take the trail left, descending the precipitous rock slope to Merritt Lake and the many excellent campsites in the open woods of its east shore.

From the lake the trail snakes down the spine of a buttress, mostly tree-shaded, and in fall a mushroom hunter's glory even though the lower reaches tend to be dry and dusty. At 3 miles from Merritt Lake the hiker reaches US 2, having hiked close to 12 miles. This one-way trip requires having some means, such as a car shuttle, to reach the car parked on road #2717.

Round trip to lookout 8 miles
Allow 6 hours
High point 6200 feet
Elevation gain 1700 feet
Best August through October
One day or backpack

Mountain goats near Alpine Lookout

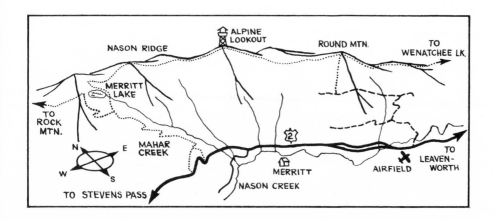

25   LARCH LAKE

An easy but long backpack trip into the very heart of the hills east of Stevens Pass, to a delightful rock-rimmed basin at the head of a long, curved mountain meadow. Here groves of alpine larch turn glorious gold in late September.

Drive on US 2 about half-way (10 miles) between Merritt and Leavenworth. Turn west 2 miles to Chiwaukum Campground of Wenatchee National Forest; trail begins a few hundred yards past campground.

Through the deep woods along Chiwaukum Creek the trail follows the easy grade set by the stream. The several trail junctions are well-marked: side trails go to the right at 2½ and 4½ miles, to the left at 5 and 6½ miles. The trail steepens then and ascends with switchbacks to ¾-mile-long Chiwaukum Lake. The Chiwaukum Mountains, 8000 feet high, range north and south a mile or so up-valley. Fishing and camping are attractions here, but for real isolation visit Larch Lake, 11 trail miles from the nearest road.

At the upper end of Chiwaukum Lake the way meets a side trail, right (an alternate access route via McCue Ridge and Merritt), then winds across a marshy ½ mile to enter Ewing Basin. At the far end of this 2-mile meadow is a round cirque lake in a setting of larches, providing boundless camping possibilities. A tried-and-proven—and recommended—backpack plan, however, is to camp 2 nights at Chiwaukum Lake,

spending a day in a side trip to explore the Larch Lake surroundings.

Approximately 4 miles of the trail and the entire eastern half of Chiwaukum Lake are privately owned.

Round trip 23 miles
Allow 2 or 3 days
High point 6150 feet
Elevation gain 3800 feet
Best mid-July through September
Backpack

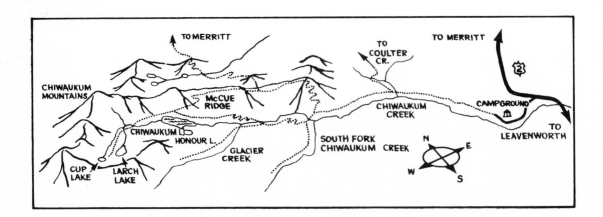

Larch Lake and Ewing Basin

26 ENCHANTMENT LAKES

Granite pinnacles of the Cashmere Crags fence a valley pocket of tiny lakes; wild and splendid scenery, rich reward for a long hike.

Drive on US 2 to Leavenworth. At the west side of town, turn south on the Icicle Creek road. Watch for Icicle Island Camp, about 5 miles. An inconspicuous sign, "Snow Creek Trail", is about 200 yards beyond. Park on the cutoff road nearby.

The trail is good, often quite wide, and not muddy, despite heavy horse traffic. No chugging motors mar the scene—the trail is closed to scooters. Switchbacks almost all the way. At 2 miles is the Snow Creek Wall—800 vertical feet of solid granite much used by rock climbers. At 5 miles is Nada Lake, a good turnaround point for beginning hikers. For backpackers there are many small campsites here, with such improvements as tables, toilets, etc.

The farther a hiker has the will and strength to go, the better; the scenery improves with every step. Another 1¾ miles to Snow Lakes, at 5700 feet, dominated by Mt. Temple on the north and Mt. McClellan on the south, both 8400 feet high. At the junction between the two lakes is a large camping area. At the upper end of the lakes is a small campsite. Here the trail ends.

The water level in Snow Lakes rises and falls frequently, resulting in a slimy no-man's-land periphery. This unlovely feature is due to the water-control system installed to provide a steady flow of suitable water for the Leavenworth Fish Hatchery. A valve under the deepest part of upper Snow Lake lets water out toward Snow Creek like a horizontal waterfall, quite spectacular. The valve is open in some degree most of the time. The beauty of Snow Lakes is therefore variable. Snow Lake trail passes alternately through Wenatchee National Forest and private land.

To get into the really good country, take a climbers' trail another 2½ miles beyond and 2000 feet above the end of Snow Lake trail. Cross a footlog and follow a foot-beaten track up through the wilds to Enchantment Lakes. Glass-clear lakes of modest size adorn every pocket and glacier-gouged basin of a high plateau of granite smoothed and scratched long ago by the nearly-vanished Snow Creek Glacier. In this exotic rock-bound setting, rimmed around with spires and towers, are innumerable campsites and endless opportunities for roaming.

Round trip 18 miles
Allow 7-10 hours in
High point 7700 feet
Elevation gain 6200 feet
Best August and September
Backpack

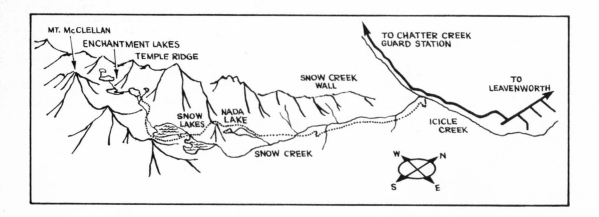

Nada Lake below, Snow Lakes above, and Mt. McClellan on the skyline.

27   LAKE CAROLINE

Six miles of easy super-trail, then up, up, and away for 2 miles which gain 2400 feet. Rewarding views from the alpine country enclosing two secluded lakes which share a ridge with 8520-foot Cashmere Mountain.

Drive on US 2 to Leavenworth, turn south onto Icicle Creek road at west end of town. Drive 14 miles to Eight Mile Creek Campground, at which parking space is ample. Trail begins ½ mile upstream at a super-bridge for horse and man across the Icicle River.

The Eight Mile Creek trail ascends easy grades through the woods, taking a right fork at 3 miles, to Little Eight Mile Lake, a pond below the main lake (campsite here). Branching off to the right, the trail to Lake Caroline climbs the forested hillside **very** steeply (switchbacks notwithstanding) to break out into flowered meadows before reaching the lake. Mile-and-a-half-high mountains are seen in profusion between the trees and from the meadows of the last mile. At Lake Caroline, in "silver forest" (standing dead trees) camps are good, but small and not as attractive as those at Little Caroline Lake, an easy ½ mile farther.

Above Little Caroline Lake is fine alpine country. The larch-sprinkled ridge (colorful in late September) rising south of the lake gives superb views of Mt. Stuart and the Stuart Range. Beautiful meadows sweep upward onto Cashmere Mountain.

A one-way trip can be made by tracing a somewhat obscure, poorly maintained trail through Windy Pass west of Cashmere Mountain, then downstream, joining the Trout Lake trail, and so returning to Icicle Creek, crossing on a footbridge near Chatter Guard Station, 9 road-miles from the starting point.

Round trip 16 miles
Allow 12 hours
High point 5900 feet
Elevation gain 4000 feet
Best July through September
Backpack

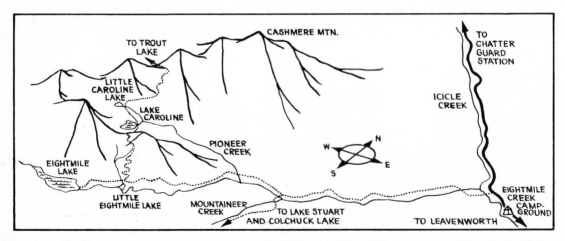

Eight Mile Creek from the ridge above Little Caroline Lake. Mount Stuart in the distance

28   LAKE MARY

A quiet lake in secluded alpine country where one can roam the lonesome mountains enjoying rocks, heather, pools, flowers, snow patches and spectacular vistas of other lakes and mountains. Reached only by a long, rough trudge and thus not crowded.

Drive on US 2 to Leavenworth; turn south onto Icicle Creek Road at west side of town. Drive some 25 miles to Rock Island Campground, cross the river on a concrete bridge and go upstream approximately 2 more miles on a new road to the proposed Black Pine Campground. Roadside parking. Trail at end of road is marked.

Icicle Creek sets the course, which crosses many tributary streams, each with a campsite. Side trails, left about 1½ miles, lead to French Creek and French Ridge Lookout. About 4 miles, turn right on Frosty Creek Trail. This trail crosses Icicle Creek in ¼ mile and then mounts very steeply through deep woods—a long, waterless, 4-mile stretch—until a short spur trail, right, at 7½ miles, ducks down to Lake Margaret, hidden in the woods.

The truly alpine meadows and mountain tops appear as 7400-foot Frosty Pass is reached, at 9.1 miles. Forming one side of the pass is Snowgrass Mountain, and the route turns right, toward it, about ¼ mile on the Wildhorse Creek Trail, then turns right again along the flanks of the mountain to drop down to Lake Mary, about 9½ miles from the starting point.

A tough trip; but a rest-day ramble of the surrounding high country will be remembered just as long. Over a little pass 1½ miles is Upper Florence Lake. Beyond it another mile is Ladies' Pass, overlooking Lake Flora and Lake Brigham. Rumor has it that the lakes in the group are named for Brigham Young and his wives. Except for "Margaret" and "Mary" none are included among the names of at least his first 19 wives, so the story may be a fabrication.

From Ladies' Pass another side trip is to austere, rockbound Lake Edna, on Cape Horn's east ridge. A short ascent of a very obvious trail from Ladies' Pass leads over a shoulder of Cape Horn, to a steep and rocky scramble to the 7300-foot summit. A full-circle panorama is displayed, including the Wenatchee Mountains, the Stuart Range, Icicle Ridge, the Chiwaukum Mountains, the countless valleys in between. Right next door is Grindstone Mountain, 7500 feet, and on the other side is Snowgrass. Unlimited camping below all these passes and at all lakes.

The expedition can be varied by returning down Chatter Creek or extended with a hike out to US 2 at Chiwaukum Creek, Merritt, or Stevens Pass, if transportation arrangements can be made.

Round trip 19 miles
Allow 3 days
High point 7400 feet   **Best in August**
Elevation gain 4000 feet   **Backpack**

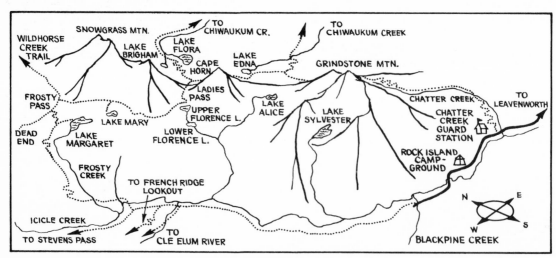

**Trail between Lake Mary and Upper Florence Lake. Grindstone Mountain
on the left and Mount Stuart in the distance**

29 DAVIS PEAK

A long, hot hike in open forest, repaid by views of the Snoqualmie peaks, Mt. Daniel, and forests of the Waptus Valley from a lookout peak overlooking the Salmon la Sac region. The eastern slopes of the Cascades often have sunshine while the westside peaks are lost in clouds, so start this trail in the early morning before the sun becomes too hot.

Drive north from Cle Elum 24 miles on State Highway 903 and continue into Wenatchee National Forest to about 2 miles past Salmon la Sac. Cross Paris Creek bridge, go 500 feet, turn left down past some private residences. Beyond the last cabin avoid the obvious road which curves to the right and down the hill. Instead, at the center of the curve turn left over the bank to another roadway (marked by a small sign "Bridge Trail") which leads to a parking area above a bridge across the Cle Elum River.

Trail starts by crossing the bridge, goes about ¼ mile, then comes out on a logging road on private property. Follow the road straight ahead, watching closely for the trail on the left. After leaving the logging road, the way is through thick forest for a full mile, in the course of which the trail reenters National Forest land and commences relentless switchbacks due north up the mountainside. Around the 2-mile mark the trees thin, allowing views east and south. A section of private land is reached about 2½ miles; the trail zig-zags over it.

At 5 miles the lookout building can be seen across a deep valley. The trail traverses the valley head, leaves private property, and then, still with switchbacks, ascends to the lookout. A wide view is offered over the Salmon la Sac area, the Wenatchee Mountains, the Cle Elum valley, and mountains, mountains, mountains. The crest of Davis Peak is shaped like the shoe of a westward-running horse, with the lookout set on one of the heel tips and Opal Lake on the other. A trail goes west along the edge of the cliffs to the true summit, West Point, at the "toe" of the horseshoe, from which the view is across Waptus Lake to Dutch Miller Gap, 10 crow-miles away.

No water available except at the very start.

Round trip 11 miles
Allow 8 hours
High point 6426 feet
Elevation gain 3900 feet
Best May-June, September-October
One day

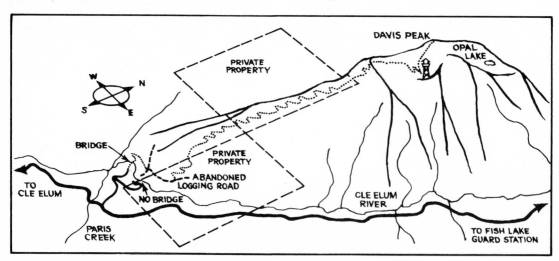

Trail to Davis Peak

A short hike on the sunny side of the mountains to a high pass and fine viewpoint. Old mines, unusual rocks, and an off-trail lake add to the interest.

Drive north from Cle Elum on State Highway 903. The paved road ends at Salmon la Sac Resort. Continue about 10 miles on a rough Forest Service road to an aged cabin that stands on the right side of the road, a few hundred feet beyond the Fish Lake Guard Station. Parking on north side of building. Sign marks start of trail.

After an easy first mile, crossing one or two streams where the hiker can reach water to add to his load, and taking the left fork at the 1-mile marker, the trail climbs steeply for the second mile. As elevation is gained trees become thinner and views become better. Shortly after the trail comes out on an open hillside at about 2 miles the trail forks again: a sharp left goes directly to the pass; the right fork goes up quite steeply to an abandoned mine from which flows an abundant and ice-cold stream, the only water between the trail beginning and ½ mile beyond the pass. From this treasure a path traverses to the north and rejoins the main trail in a meadow. Passing some interesting rock formations and old mine diggings, the route ascends to the pass. The Cle Elum River valley and Fish Lake are down below, and across the valley, northward a little, are glimpses of Mt. Daniel and Cathedral Rock. To the east The Cradle (7465 feet), only 2 miles away, is seen directly across a deep valley. Easy climbs to vantage points on either side of the pass lead to even better views.

Sprite Lake is on the east side of the ridge and ½ mile south, at approximately the same elevation as the pass. A side trip to this tiny round lake can follow natural benches across open meadow where there is small danger of getting lost. If in doubt, stay high until the lake can be seen below.

Over the pass and down the other side the trail goes, to join other trails which can be used for a lengthy backpack trip or for a long day's circuit, coming out at Scatter Creek Camp, 1½ miles south of the starting point.

For almost a mile on both sides of the pass the trail crosses private land. Sprite Lake also is privately owned.

Round trip 7 miles
Allow 5 hours
High point 6100 feet
Elevation gain 2700 feet
Best June through October
One day

Sprite Lake and Cradle Mountain

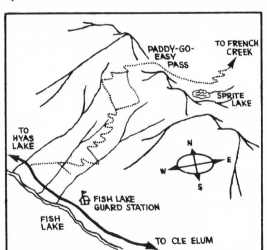

A large blue lake at the head of a broad meadow, seeming to hug the base of 7986-foot Mt. Daniel, highest peak in King County.

Drive north from Cle Elum on State Highway 903 past Salmon la Sac Resort; continue on rough Forest Service road past Fish Lake to road's end, 33 miles from Cle Elum. Turn left on narrow road ¼ mile to a picnic area and space to park. Sign marks trail.

A new footbridge crosses the Cle Elum River. Beyond is good walking in dense forest, shady and cool. A small brook at 1 mile provides water. Here an abandoned trail may still be evident in switchbacks up to the left, but the main trail continues straight ahead at a more moderate grade. On the border between forest and alpine meadows, the trail skirts Squaw Lake, a good turnaround point for a short afternoon.

A new section of trail continues from Squaw Lake north along the side of a ridge to the base of Cathedral Rock, at 3 miles, providing excellent views of the upper Salmon la Sac valley, Mt. Stuart, Mt. Daniel, and Cathedral Rock itself. After crossing the ridge top the trail becomes the permanent route of the Cascade Crest Trail and descends a steep hillside into thickening woods which allow occasional glimpses of the destination, large and sparkling Deep Lake. A high, thin waterfall drops into the lake, and beyond it rises Mt. Daniel, whose dry, pinkish slopes contrast with the dark angular walls of Cathedral Rock.

The trail approaches Deep Lake near a small but clean campsite on the east shore. Other comfortable campsites, farther down-lake, are larger, but since the lake is popular with trail riders, some may be horsy in odor and decoration.

South of Deep Lake a wide, flat, meadow opens out—ample pasture for horses, and fenced at strategic points across the southern edge. The Cascade Crest Trail continues through, and south along Spinola Creek to Waptus Lake.

Round trip 10 miles
Allow 8 hours
High point 5500 feet
Elevation gain to Deep Lake 2000 feet,
on return 1000 feet
Best June through October
One day or backpack

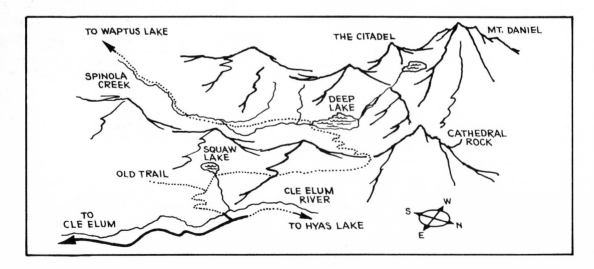

Deep Lake and a shoulder of Mount Daniel

32   MARMOT LAKE

High under the banded cliffs of Terrace Mountain, in the scenic backcountry near the Cascade Divide, lies uncrowded Marmot Lake.

Drive north from Cle Elum 33 miles on State Highway 903, entering Wenatchee National Forest and continuing to the end of the road. Ample parking space. Signs indicate Cascade Crest Trail.

Follow the Crest Trail 1½ miles up the dwindling Cle Elum River toward the lower end of Hyas Lake. The sandy beach and a chance to swim or fish attract many people to the campground here. The hiker in search of solitude may take heart: the human population decreases rapidly as the distance from the road increases. Hike along the east shore for 1½ miles to the upper end of the lake (good campsite here), then continue up the valley, pausing to look back at the view of the lake and of Mount Daniel and Mount Hinman. Pass a side trail, right, to Tuck Lake and to Granite Mountain summits, via a climbers' route. At Deception Pass, 5 miles, leave the Crest Trail—which continues north through the pass—and go left on the Marmot Lake Trail.

The well-defined trail to Marmot Lake has a moderate grade and is relatively good, although between the 1- and 2-mile markers some mud, rocks, and brush hamper the foot-traveler, and it is wise to pay close attention to the trail, especially as it passes through the meadow along here. Just beyond the 3-mile marker the trail ends; the last half-mile or so is only a fishermen's track, very steep but not otherwise difficult. So long as one always goes up, keeping to the route presents no problem.

Marmot Lake is large and roundish, framed on two sides by cliffs 1000 feet high. The best camp spots are about ¼ mile around the shore toward the south from the access trail.

Deception Pass (and Marmot Lake) can also be approached from the Stevens Pass Highway, by either of two routes. One, a 12½-mile journey up Surprise Creek and then south along the Cascade Crest Trail, starts in the little town of Scenic, 6 miles west of Stevens Pass. The other, a 12-mile ascent of Deception Creek, starts at Deception Falls 2 miles west of Scenic. These two approaches through Snoqualmie National Forest can be combined into a loop trip.

Round trip via Hyas Lake 17 miles
Allow 10 hours
High point 4900 feet
Elevation gain 1470 feet
Best July through October
Backpack

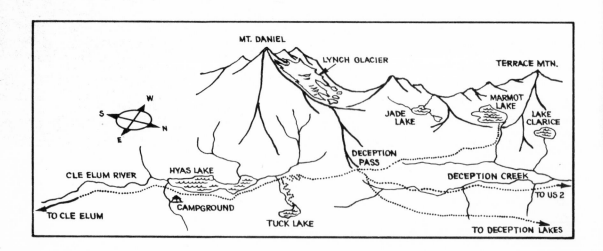

Air view of Marmot Lake, Mount Daniel (left) and Mount Hinman (right)

33　LONG'S PASS

A high pass in the Wenatchee Mountains, looking in one direction to the Teanaway River and the cirque-rim Esmerelda Peaks, in the other across the long valley of Ingalls Creek to the south wall of 9470-foot Mt. Stuart, second-highest nonvolcanic peak in the state. Often when the Cascade crest is being drenched this rain-shadowed area is sunny and clear, though perhaps windy, with dramatic clouds around.

Drive on US 10 to 4 miles east of Cle Elum, turn north on US 97 and go 5 miles, turn left on Teanaway road. Following "North Fork Teanaway" signs at all forks, drive 23 miles (the last 10 on gravel) to road end. Beyond the parking lot extends an abandoned mining roadway officially closed to 4-wheel vehicles. This is the trail. (County Line trail #1394.)

The "trail" climbs a short valley step where splendid waterfalls make the trip worthwhile even if it ends here. The way flattens above the falls, passing alternately through lush meadows at riverside and rock-garden meadows on buttresses; the rugged face of Esmerelda looks down from the opposite shore.

Immediately after crossing a tributary creek at ½ mile, the route leaves the stream and turns right uphill on the first side road, marked "Ingalls Lake." At a fork ¼ mile up, a sign points to "Ingalls Lake" left, "Turnpike Creek Trail" right. The right fork, which leads to Long's Pass, crosses a creek and rounds a switchback. Just at this point a miner's bulldozer track goes straight uphill and a footpath takes off to the right. Take the footpath; from here the route is genuine trail all the way except for a short stretch of the bulldozer track high up and crossings of the track elsewhere. Stick with the trail; it is nicer and easier, switchbacking up through arid-land meadows and alpine trees. Except for snowmelt, there is no water within 500 vertical feet of the pass on either side.

Fine views from the pass. Rockhounds should be prepared to stagger home under maximum loads. Botanists find the rare plants of the "serpentine barrens" here of unusual interest.

An excellent campsite lies up the Teanaway about ¼ mile beyond the Long's Pass turnoff. In the wide, green, flat meadows beside the river, less than 1 mile from parking, a basecamp can be set up for several one-day hikes to Ingalls Lake, Ingalls Pass, and the head of the Teanaway valley.

Round trip 4 miles
Allow 5 hours
High point 6000 feet
Elevation gain 1500 feet
Best June 15 to July 15
One day

Mount Stuart from near Long's Pass

34   RED TOP MOUNTAIN

An easy hike on sunny, dry Teanaway Ridge, a paradise for the rockhounds who gather agates, jasper, geodes, and crystals there. Others come for the impressive view of Stuart. Trail often is open by the end of May.

Drive north from Teanaway on US 97 to first forest road beyond Mineral Springs Resort; turn left on this, then right on the Blue Creek Road. Go about 6 miles to road-end parking area and trail take-off. (About halfway up keep left, avoiding the Hovey Creek Road, thereafter keep right.)

The road climbs to the top of Teanaway Ridge, and the left-hand trail follows the ridge crest north for the remaining ½ mile to Red Top Lookout at the summit. The viewpoint commands the North Fork Teanaway River; Iron Peak hides Long's Pass from view, but Mt. Stuart shows up beautifully. In the southwest distance Mt. Rainier can be distinguished. Across Swauk Prairie southeast lie Ellensburg and the Yakima Valley.

The Teanaway Ridge Trail runs north and south of the lookout for many miles, more than one would want to attempt in a short day trip. North 200 yards from the lookout the Blue Creek Trail branches off to the right, descending back to the road. (About ¼ mile along this side trail is a spring, the only source of water on the trip.) North from the lookout ½ mile, a side trail branches to the left and down Indian Creek 5 miles to the North Fork Teanaway.

About 1 mile through alpine meadows from the summit the trail enters the "Battlefield", a criss-cross of trenches dug by rockhounds in search of red and blue agates. The entire ridge top is a happy hunting ground for lapidarists. Local stores and motels cater to these hobbyists, and the Cle Elum Chamber of Commerce issues a folder of information and maps (useful to hikers as well).

Walk as far as desired—perhaps 2 miles, to the Hovey Creek Trail—then return. One-way hikes depend on a non-hiking driver willing to meet the party at the intersection of Blue Creek Trail with the Blue Creek Road (total 1½ miles), or at the intersection of the Hovey Creek Trail with the Hovey Divide Road (total 2½ miles). A short loop trip of approximately 1 mile can be made by taking the righthand trail out to the ridge top junction north of the lookout, then turning south on the trail past the lookout. This route is over little-used section of scenic trail across the face of the cliffs below the lookout; a reasonably good trail, but not recommended for the faint-hearted or acrophobic.

Round trip 4 miles
Allow 2 hours
High point 5361 feet
Elevation gain 500 feet
Best in June
One day

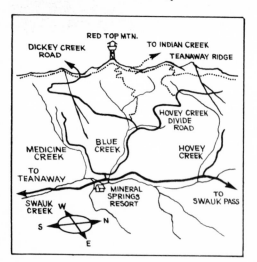

Red Top Mountain

35   BERTHA MAY LAKES

An easy trail through pleasant forests, connecting four little lakes. A thousand feet higher, paralleling the trail, is Sawtooth Ridge, with a lookout sitting atop its east end.

Drive to Ashford on State Highway 705, continue straight ahead (east) about 2½ miles to Kernahan Road, where there is a Snoqualmie National Forest sign. Turn right 1½ miles to junction with Skate Creek Road; then turn left and continue 2.7 miles to a junction. Take the right fork, Berry Creek Road, for 4.2 miles; turn right onto the Cora Lake Road and go increasingly uphill for 1.6 miles. Just after crossing Big Creek watch for trail sign on left, "Big Creek Trail". Park near here wherever the road is wide enough.

Pretty little Cora Lake is ½ mile from the road, with High Rock Lookout perched like a Japanese garden house 1700 feet above. At the lake are picnic tables, fireplaces, toilets, and a vandalized shelter.

Continue up the wooded ridge to the right from Cora Lake; in ½ mile is a junction with trail, left, which goes south to the Berry Creek Road. The route goes up a little, down a little, for 1½ miles, along the base of the geologically interesting, almost vertical cliffs of Sawtooth Ridge, then descends to blue-green Granite Lake. The campsites here have been much used but are still attractive.

Less than ½ mile farther is Bertha May Lake, also providing excellent camps. Still another, much smaller, lake—the other of the two Bertha May Lakes—lies a short distance downstream to the north.

All these lakes are charming, surrounded by hillsides of leaf-green and rock-gray, with little rivulets cascading into the jewel-clear water. Ideal destinations for a beginners' backpack trip.

For a famous view of Mt. Rainier, visit High Rock Lookout. Drive to the end of Berry Creek Road; a sign marks the start of the 1½ mile path, well-maintained, which climbs very steeply through open woods and flowers, and, in late August, through huckleberries, to the ridge crest. In summer, firewatchers are on duty.

Round trip to lakes 6 miles
Allow 4½ hours
High point 4500 feet
Elevation gain 1000 feet
Best June through November
One day or backpack

Round trip to lookout 3 miles
Allow 3 hours
High point 5687 feet
Elevation gain 1500 feet
Best July 15 to October 15
One day

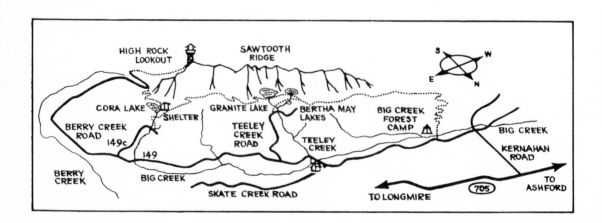

High Rock Lookout

A native of long ago was fond of hunting in this meadowland at the head of Tahoma Creek, where flowers and glaciers meet. A famous panorama from here of the South Tahoma Glacier on Rainier's southwest side.

Drive to Mount Rainier National Park, Nisqually entrance, and turn left on the West Side Road. Go 4 miles to Tahoma Creek Campground. Park in a campsite if the space will be wanted later for camping; otherwise park at roadside. Trail, signed, takes off from back of campground.

Climb rather sharply along Tahoma Creek for 2 miles to junction with the Wonderland Trail. Take the right branch, which almost immediately crosses Tahoma Creek on a footbridge frequently washed out by meltwater floods. Just beyond the bridge, on open valley-train barrens, is an unobstructed view of Glacier Island, a cleaver between two rivers of ice which formerly was actually surrounded by the two glaciers.

After passing a last mile through forest, the trail comes to a shelter, a good camping place. Across from the shelter a side trail left leads ¾ mile to the very pretty Mirror Lakes, which were pictured on the 3¢ stamp of the National Park series.

Beyond the shelter are the flowers, streams, and ponds of Indian Henrys Hunting Ground, a fine place for rambling and for looking upward to the glaciers of Rainier.

For variety, a loop trip totalling 9½ miles can be made by descending the Kautz Creek Trail to the Nisqually-Paradise road at the Kautz Creek Roadside Exhibit.

Round trip 7½ miles
Allow 5 hours
High point 5500 feet
Elevation gain 2300 feet
Best August through October
One day or backpack

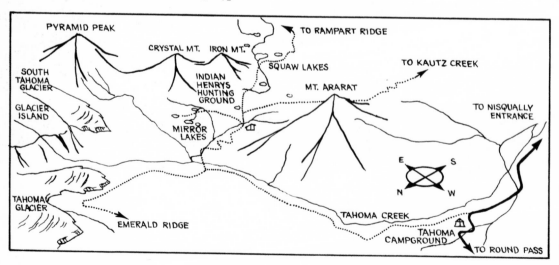

Indian Henrys Hunting Ground and Mount Rainier

37 GOBBLERS KNOB

Wide trail to a lookout with unobstructed view over Klapatche Ridge, South Puyallup River, Emerald Ridge, and Indian Henrys Hunting Ground, and up Tahoma Glacier to Rainier's summit. Other mountains on the far horizon: Hood, Adams, and St. Helens.

Drive to Mount Rainier National Park, turn left 1 mile beyond the Nisqually River entrance and drive north 6 miles on the West Side Road to Round Pass parking area and the start of the trail. (Just beyond the parking is a viewpoint and the memorial to U.S. Marines killed in a 1946 airplane crash on South Tahoma Glacier.)

The excellent trail is city-park-like, worn smooth by many feet, and two people wide. For a mile it winds along a very easy grade to 26-acre Lake George, surrounded by dense forest. Crowded camping here, and trail shelter. Swimming is possible.

Beyond the lake another 1½ miles the trail climbs a bit more obviously, but still gently, passing a junction with a poor side trail, left, which goes steeply downhill a mile to Goat Lake, outside the park. (Campsites here are quieter than those at George.) Beyond the junction the trail emerges from timber and climbs to the fire lookout atop the weird cliffs of the "knob", a rock garden of phlox and juniper. Flowers are best in July; the vista of Rainier is supreme in any season. In late summer no water beyond Lake George inlet stream.

Round trip 5 miles
Allow 4 hours
High point 5000 feet
Elevation gain 1100 feet
Best July to October
One day or backpack

Above the clouds on Gobblers Knob

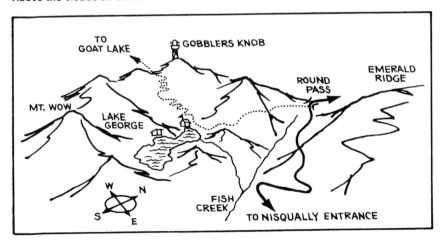

38   EMERALD RIDGE

Close under the west slopes of Rainier the grassy green of Emerald Ridge meets the sparkling white of Tahoma Glacier. As recently as 25 years ago tongues of the glacier flowed past the ridge for a mile on both sides; now the southern ice tongue has completely retreated and the northern one extends no more than 1/4 mile past the ridge's highest point, leaving valley-train barrens that set off the emerald of the ridge.

Drive to Nisqually entrance of Mount Rainier National Park, turn left on the West Side Road and drive north about 7 miles, through Round Pass, and on down to parking area near the South Puyallup River Bridge. Trail takes off to the right, about 100 yards south of the bridge.

Splendid giant cedars dignify the dense forests along the South Puyallup River, where the trail at first progresses upward by an easy grade. After 1 mile it steepens somewhat, and soon thereafter passes beneath an immense cliff of columnar andesite formed by the shrinkage of cooling lava. This display of many-sided columns, several hundred feet high and almost a thousand feet long, is one of the finest in the park.

At 1½ miles is a junction with the Wonderland Trail which comes in at left (after zigzagging down from St. Andrews and Klapatche Parks). The Emerald Ridge route continues to the right on the Wonderland Trail for another 2 miles through green turf where mountain goats are sometimes seen. At the easternmost point is a vista down on the blue-whiteness of Tahoma Glacier and up its cold slopes to Tokaloo Rock and the Puyallup Cleaver. Off to the right across the gravelly bed of the deceased glacier is the rock eminence of Glacier Island.

If a longer return trip is desired, continue south on the Wonderland Trail and descend Tahoma Creek to the West Side Road, or go north on this trail to meet the Klapatche Ridge Trail (see Klapatche Park description) and follow it to the road.

Round trip 7 miles
Allow 5 hours
High point 5700 feet
Elevation gain 2200 feet
Best July through October
One day

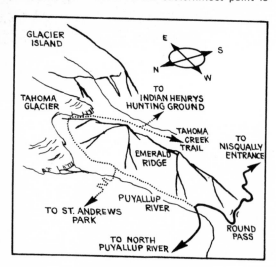

Emerald Ridge and the Tahoma Glacier

39   KLAPATCHE PARK

A stunning view of Rainier's Sunset Amphitheatre makes this easy walk a consensus all-time favorite in Mount Rainier National Park: through forest and meadows west of the Puyallup Glacier to alpine wildflower gardens and heather slopes surrounding a miniscule pond in Klapatche Park.

Drive to Nisqually River entrance of Rainier National Park. Turn left on West Side Road, drive approximately 10 miles to St. Andrews Creek and a sign on the right indicating Klapatche Ridge trail. Parking nearby.

The excellent trail climbs through heavy timber gradually but steadily, then follows the crest of the ridge to open suddenly into the Klapatche meadow at 2½ miles. No water along the ridge. At Klapatche Park there is a well across the lake from a trail shelter. The shelter is usually occupied, especially on weekends. A junction here with the Wonderland Trail makes a good turnaround point.

For a side trip to 6000-foot St. Andrews Park continue to the right along the Wonderland Trail another ¾ mile. From the trail Sunset Amphitheatre at the head of the Puyallup Glacier is seen at its best; an overlook gives an unrestricted panorama across the great canyon. The colorful meadows and peaceful tarns of St. Andrews are at their finest in fall. Mountain goats may sometimes be seen in summer on upper ridges of Klapatche and St. Andrews.

Still one more extra mile of trail leads to the divide crest south of St. Andrews Park, and a view over the South Puyallup River valley to Emerald Ridge, to Gobblers Knob off to the west, and of Tahoma Glacier sweeping up to the east. From the crest, wander freely without trail along the ridge toward Tokaloo Rock and the mountain, past snow-melt ponds and flowery benches. If a loop trip is desired, continue south from the divide crest to the South Puyallup River Trail, then west along it 1½ miles to the West Side Road (see Emerald Ridge description).

Round trip 5 miles
Allow 3 hours
High point 5500 feet
Elevation gain 1800 feet
Best July 15 through October
One day or backpack

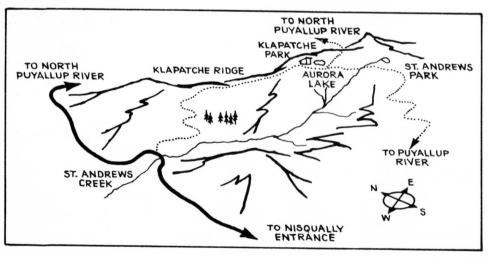

Aurora Lake and Mount Rainier

Quick and easy walk on good trail to the saddle between Pinnacle Peak and Plummer Peak. Pleasant alpine country dominated by the huge bulk of Rainier, several miles away but seeming even closer.

Drive on State Highway 706 east from Ashford, entering Mount Rainier National Park at the Nisqually entrance. Pass Longmire, take Stevens Canyon Road to Reflection Lakes; park in the first parking area, on left side of road. A bit of searching is needed to find the trail, across the road from the lot. The sign is not at all prominent.

The trail is wide enough at first for talkative hikers to walk side by side, then narrows to the conventional Indian-file width. Good condition all the way, but crosses some treacherous snow slopes early in the season. The terrain is quite open, providing in clear weather grand views over Reflection Lakes and Paradise Park to ice streams and rock buttresses sweeping upward to the 14,410-foot summit of the mountain the Indians called Tahoma.

At the saddle the trail dwindles away in alpine flowers. Experienced climbers can ascend Pinnacle from here. Hikers should confine their explorations to the delightful alpine trees on the rounder top of Plummer, 6300 feet high, or rest at the saddle, a respectable 5900 feet above the sea.

Round trip to saddle 2.6 miles
Allow 2½ hours
High point 5900 feet
Elevation gain 1000 feet
Best July 15 to October 15
One day

Mount Rainier and trail to Pinnacle-Plummer Saddle

41   PARADISE ICE CAVES

A rare opportunity to get right next to a glacier, and, if the weather permits, to explore the ice caves under it and walk around on top of it. (Not open every year, and if so only in late summer.)

Drive on State Highway 706, entering Mount Rainier National Park from the southwest, and continue to Paradise parking area. Trail, marked with a sign, begins just west of the Ranger Station. Always check with the ranger before starting out; conditions vary a great deal.

To protect against erosion, the trail is paved for the first few hundred yards and, like other popular trails in national parks, is well-maintained throughout its length. However, the last half-mile is only a trace and is often through snow; sturdy cleated shoes are therefore advisable. Warm clothing should be carried, too; under the glacier the climate is always cold and wet.

From the Ranger Station the trail goes right, to the junction beyond Myrtle Falls, then right again on the Mazama Ridge trail to cross the Paradise River below Sluiskin Falls and ascend Mazama Ridge to a junction with the Skyline Trail at 1½ miles. Continue left along the Skyline Trail up the ridge for ½ mile before branching to the right at the rustic sign, "Ice Caves". From here on what path there is has been made by the tramping of many feet; when snow covers the way, flags may be placed by rangers to mark the route to the snout of the Stevens Glacier.

When bare, blue ice is exposed, experienced hikers may safely walk a short way out onto the flat surface of the glacier, always keeping a sharp eye for crevasses. However, **never venture onto snow-covered glaciers;** there may be hidden crevasses.

Melt streams running out from underneath the glacier (the source of Stevens Creek) form great caverns; in seasons when the snow has disappeared sufficiently from around the openings it is possible to enter the chilly depths. On sunny days the outer caves are suffused with a beautiful blue light filtered through the ice, but a flashlight is required to completely explore the extensive, many-branched inner caves. Some years the caves are not open: heavy snows may cover the entrances; warm weather may collapse the ceilings.

A variation can be made on the return trip by continuing north (right) up the Skyline Trail some ½ mile, then going west (left) down into Edith Creek Basin to the starting point.

Round trip 6 miles
Allow 3 to 5 hours
High point 6300 feet
Elevation gain 900 feet
Best late July through September
One day

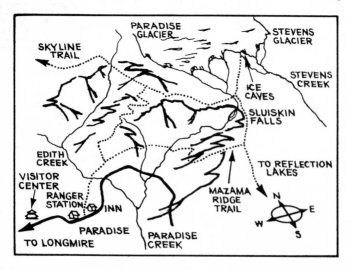

Paradise Ice Caves

42　MORAINE PARK

A near view of Mount Rainier's north wall set off by flower-and-grass-carpeted meadows, or by blazing fall colors, plus intimate closeups of one of the mountain's largest glaciers.

Drive on the Carbon River road to Mount Rainier National Park. Park at Ipsut Creek Campground, road's end. Start from the campground on the well-marked Wonderland Trail.

The way lies along an abandoned road through superb forests for 1.9 miles. Then turn left on marked trail and cross the Carbon River on a bridge. In another 2 miles the trail passes close to the 3400-foot snout of the Carbon Glacier, the lowest in the park. Rock flour muddies the stream which emerges from under the terminal ice; boulders cover the surface and sometimes tumble down the ice front — keep clear!

The trail parallels the Carbon Glacier, ascending steeply on moraines, beside cliffs and waterfalls, 2 more miles to the flower-spread meadows of 6000-foot Moraine Park. Excellent views of Carbon Glacier and of Willis Wall, rising 3600 feet above its head. Enormous and frequent avalanches from the summit icecap thunder down the wall.

For a somewhat longer trip or for an overnight stay, continue 1 more mile from Moraine Park; the trail climbs to a divide and then drops 300 feet to a shelter cabin and campsite at Mystic Lake, set in its own meadow at the base of Old Desolate.

The meadow-and-scree highway of lower Curtis Ridge virtually requires the ambitious walker to make a close up inspection of the mountain.

Round trip 10 miles
Allow 6 hours
High point 6000 feet
Elevation gain 3000 feet
Best July 15 through September
One day or backpack

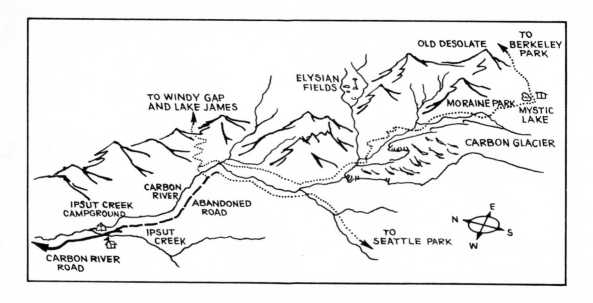

Willis Wall, north face of Mount Rainier, from Moraine Park

43   TOLMIE PEAK

Easy walk to a fire lookout with a grand view dominated by the northwest side of Rainier and its Carbon, Russell, and North Mowich Glaciers.

Drive toward Mount Rainier National Park on the Carbon River road. A quarter-mile or so beyond the Carbon River Bridge take the right fork. Continue past famous and panoramic views of barren logged country into the blessed greenery of Rainier Park, and on to the main Mowich Lake parking area.

The trail skirts the forested west shore of Mowich Lake, then climbs to Ipsut Pass, at 1½ miles, where it divides. (Take a side trip 50 yards to the right to look over the pass down into the Ipsut Creek valley.) To the left the trail continues in the open to Eunice Lake at 2½ miles, a nice spot for lunching while admiring the spectacular view of Rainier across the water. Blueberries in late summer. Camping and fires are prohibited in order to preserve these fragile and easily-reached meadows.

From Eunice Lake to the lookout is ¾ mile of rather steep trail. A register is deposited at the very top of the peak, 200 yards from the lookout house, to record the names of those who attain the summit. The way to the register is narrow and rocky——not suitable for small children.

Round trip 6 miles
Allow 4 hours
High point 5939 feet
Elevation gain 1000 feet
Best August and September
One day

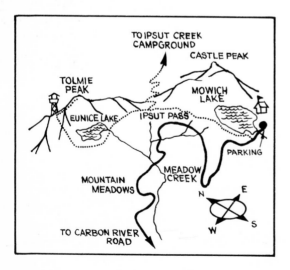

Eunice Lake and Mount Rainier at sunset

44 SPRAY PARK

One of the supreme flower gardens in Rainier National Park, with near views of ice cliffs on Ptarmigan Ridge. Pond-sprinkled meadows provide innumerable campsites, surrounding ridges invite and demand exploration.

Drive toward Mount Rainier National Park on the Carbon River Road to ¼ mile beyond the canyon bridge; take right fork, the Mowich Lake Road, to parking area at road end. Take the Wonderland Trail from the parking lot; at less than ¼ mile Spray Park Trail branches left.

The trail contours through subalpine forest, up a little, down a little. Just off the trail at 1½ miles is Eagle Cliff, offering an impressive view of Rainier. A steep 600-foot drop here: watch the children! At 2 miles a side trail right crosses a footlog and goes .3 miles to a vantage point below fan-shaped Spray Falls. The main trail now switchbacks up some 600 feet in about ½ mile and enters the meadowland of Spray Park, with Hessong Rock and Mt. Pleasant on the left and Rainier glaciers to the right, seen beyond 7800-foot Echo Rock and 8300-foot Observation Rock.

Good campsites where the trail first emerges into open country, but better ones can be found by going higher and higher. Leave the trail in the meadow below Hessong Rock, strike out past creeks, ponds, waterfalls, and ice-scratched buttresses toward Rainier; camp in any of a dozen secluded nooks. Explore the vast flowerfields, splash in waist-deep pools, seek out the hidden lake behind a moraine at the foot of Observation Rock. Late July and early August are best for flowers, but there is then too much snow for the easy roaming possible in autumn.

For another side trip, hike across the parkland and up to the saddle between Hessong Rock and Mt. Pleasant, both over 6100 feet; for further adventure, continue contouring north along Mt. Pleasant to the 6500-foot summit of Fay Peak and a look down at Mowich Lake.

For a one-way trip, if transportation is available, descend through Seattle Park to the Carbon River, perhaps making a side trip in Seattle Park to the ridge overlooking the Carbon Glacier and Willis Wall. A 3-day loop trip can be made by continuing the journey from the Carbon River up Ipsut Creek and back to the parking area at Mowich Lake.

Round trip to Spray Park 8 miles
Allow 6 hours
High point 6000 feet
Elevation gain 1300 feet
Best July through October
One day or backpack

Avalanche lilies at Spray Park

45　SUMMERLAND

Easy walk to high meadows and glacier views on the sunrise side of Rainier, with an inviting trail leading still higher to the broad panorama from Panhandle Gap.

Drive on US 410 to Mount Rainier National Park, White River entrance. Go 3 miles on Yakima Park Road to Fryingpan Creek. Parking area on right, trail beginning on left.

A veritable sidewalk (so wide and smooth is it) climbs the forested course of Fryingpan Creek to Summerland, just at tree-line, 5400 feet. Flowers, flowers, flowers strew the grassy rolling fields, nourished by streams burbling from the abutting ice. Ahead, across a sweep of tenacious low-growing plants and a wave-crest of rock is Fryingpan Glacier and the dark ruggedness of 11,117-foot Little Tahoma. To the right is Emmons Glacier and the high, melon-shaped mass of Goat Island Mountain. The glittering brilliance of Rainier dominates all.

To allow time for soaking up scenery or for more exploring, camp overnight in the parkland. A side trip to Panhandle Gap calls for an extra 2 hours or more on the zig-zaggy, 3-mile trail, and an additional 1000 feet of elevation gain. From the Gap one can see Mt. Adams, Mt. Hood, the Goat Rocks, more valleys and ridges of Mt. Rainier, and the headwater drainage of the Ohanapecosh River. This portion of the Wonderland Trail is largely snow-covered into August.

Round trip 8 miles
Allow 6 hours
High point 5700 feet
Elevation gain 1800 feet
Best July through October
One day or backpack

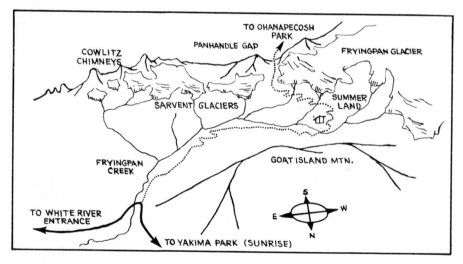

Summerland and the Emmons Glacier

46   BURROUGHS MOUNTAIN

The magnificence of Rainier and the famous glaciers and rock formations of its north side may be fully appreciated from the "platform" of the Burroughs summit. A loop trail circles the unusually broad and level mountain top, virtually barren although it provides the habitat for some unusual flowers and birds.

Drive south from Enumclaw on US 410, entering Mount Rainier National Park at the White River entrance. Drive to Sunrise, park at Yakima Park Plaza. Take the Wonderland Trail off the north side of the upper campground.

The circuit begins with a climb 500 feet up Sourdough Mountain, then turns left to Frozen Lake, a campground reservoir. Just beyond the lake the Mt. Fremont trail is passed on the right, and at the next junction the Burroughs Mountain trail goes left, ascending 300 feet to the wide, almost flat, 7000-foot summit of dry volcanic rock and cinders. (No water.) Near the center of the summit the trail branches. Go left, descending south 1/4 mile, then returning east along the dips and rises of the Yakima Park Rim Trail, which should be negotiated cautiously since snow lingers late and there are dangerous sheer cliffs below. The circle trip ends at the south side of the parking plaza. The hike is equally good in the reverse direction.

The summit has a little heather here and there and some tiny alpine flowers, among them silene acaulis, the moss campion, like a clump of green moss with tiny pink flowers. The pallid horned lark nests here. Mountain goats may be seen.

To the north is the green expanse of Grand Park, a huge lush alpine meadow. To the southwest are Willis Wall and Russell Cliff, over which pour occasional spectacular avalanches. Steamboat Prow, a wedge of rock pointing up the Emmons Glacier, is prominent across the narrow valley of Glacier Basin.

A side trip to the third and highest hump of Burroughs Mountain may be made by continuing west along the crest from the trail junction at the middle of the mountain, then leaving the trail and traveling cross-country. The view is even better from this hump, and includes a look straight down onto the Winthrop Glacier. The trail passes near the Meany Memorial, dedicated in 1936 to Dr. Edmond S. Meany, first President of the Mountaineers.

Round trip 5 miles
Allow 3 hours
High point 7350 feet
Elevation gain 950 feet
Best in August and September
One day

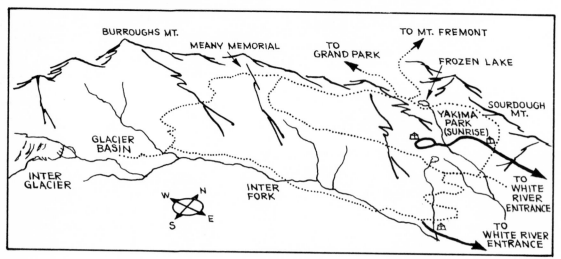

Mount Rainier from trail to Burroughs Mountain

47 NACHES PEAK

An easy loop hike on the Cascade Crest Trail circling Naches Peak, through meadows all the way. For side trips, climb to the top of the mountain or drop to Dewey Lakes for fishing and splashing. A profusion of flowers in late July, and countless small waterfalls sparkling through shrub and hummock. By September both flowers and falls have vanished, replaced by such other beauties as blueberries and autumn color.

Drive on US 410 to Chinook Pass. Park at Tipsoo Lake. Walk around the lake to the west side and up through the woods ½ mile on trail roughly paralleling the highway, to just east of the summit, where a pedestrian overpass crosses to the east portion of the loop.

Traverse steep flower slopes 1 mile to a lakelet on the left. More meadows and a gentle climb lead over a ridge, the highest point of the trip. From here it is a short and easy meadow-scramble to the 6457-foot summit of Naches Peak. The Cascade Crest Trail continues beyond the ridge to intersect the national park alternate Cascade Crest Trail at 2 miles. This intersection may have no sign; Dewey Lakes are along the Crest Trail to the left and down.

The trail sharply drops 600 feet in less than ½ mile from the junction to the two blue alpine lakes, set in meadows, rockslides, and tree-groves. The shores of the easily accessible lakes are heavily camped.

The return route is along the Cascade Crest Trail to the junction, then left, past another lakelet (campsite), and around Naches Peak, leaving Snoqualmie National Forest to enter Rainier National Park. Tipsoo Lake and the highway are regained in 2½ miles from the trail intersection.

Rewarding short strolls, suitable for toddlers and oldsters, can be made from either end of the loop trail. To walk the east segment of the trail, park at the pedestrian overpass just east of the pass summit; trail-head is marked on the east-bound side of the highway. To walk the west segment, park at Tipsoo Lake; trail begins at the outside center of the curve where the road swings around the lake—a non-obvious sign is posted a hundred feet from the roadway.

To Lakes:
Round trip 5½ miles
Allow 4 hours
High point 5900 feet
Elevation gain, 600 feet in, 700 feet out
Best late July through October
One day or backpack

To Peak:
Round trip 6 miles
Allow 6 hours
High point 6457 feet
Elevation gain 1143 feet
Best late July through October
One day or backpack

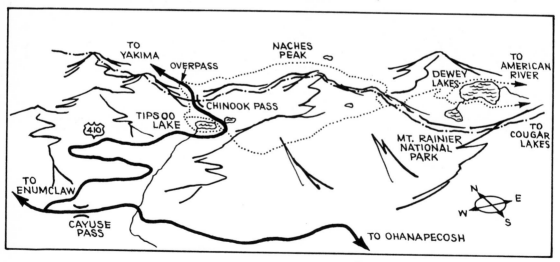

Mount Rainier, Chinook Pass Highway, and Tipsoo Lakes, from Naches Peak

48   MT. PETE

Also known as Mt. Peak or Pinnacle Peak. The modest summit of this prominent little knob at the edge of the Cascades, surrounded by flat pastureland of the White River, gives a fine view of the region north of Rainier.

Drive east from Enumclaw on US 410 about 1 mile and turn right on 284th Ave. S. E., just beyond the State Natural Resources building. At S.E. 472nd St. turn right (west) and curve around the north side of Mt. Pete, following the road about ½ mile to where it makes a right-angle turn right (north). Park at side of road. No sign, but the obvious trail begins near the corner.

The way is short but steep. No drinking water at all, so bring some or go without. The trail climbs through woods to the service road, then continues along the road a short distance to the summit, passing an interesting outcrop of columnar basalt.

Mt. Rainier dominates the scene, but equally interesting are the cows, barns, pastures, and towns of the White River valley, from near-by Enumclaw and Buckley west to Puget Sound. When smog allows, see the Olympics. Look north over little hillocks rising from the plain to Tiger Mountain and other peaks of the Issaquah Range.

The summit walk can also begin from the south side, by the gated service road. Drive from US 410 south 2.7 miles, turn right .6 mile to a small parking lot at the side of the main road across from the entrance. At a junction about ½ mile from the gate, take the right fork. The road walk is 3 miles round trip, longer than the trail but less steep.

Round trip 2 miles
Allow 2 hours
High point 1801 feet
Elevation gain 1100 feet
All seasons good
One day

35   WALLACE FALLS

Exploring an area like Wallace Falls yields
a dividends in vignettes of local history.
ut only for the observant and inquisitive mind.

Hard to believe, trekking through moccasin-
soft stillness of the woods, the life and times
that once throbbed here. The Northwest "jungle"
consumes and buries the past rapidly. One can
pass its signs totally unseeing.

The falls, part of a future state park (land
purchased but undeveloped), are visible in the
green wall north of the highway approaching
Goldbar from the west, seemingly unattainable.
Yet the hike is an easy stroll three-fourths of
the way. Only the last bit separates the men
from boys—and women from blabber-mouths
(like yours truly).

Drive east on US 2 to edge of Goldbar. Turn
left at first intersection (Standard Station) and
follow Wallace Lake signs through right turn and
Y fork (go left) 1.2 miles to Episcopal Camp
Huston sign where paved road turns sharp right.
Park on wide shoulder left of sign. A dirt road
goes left uphill for the lake and a graveled
road ahead is gated. Begin hike ascending road
behind gate. In 1/4 mile, where it turns right
to houses, go straight on an old logging road
through woods, and across a powerline clearing
1/4 mile more. It begins again with a fork. Go
left. Gradually the road ascends, switchbacks
right, and reaches a wide clearing in another
mile. The clearing is an old railroad landing and
junction with spur road connecting with Wallace

Lake road, and supports of an old trestle still
are seen.

Keep straight past the clearing. In 1 mile
is another clearing. Turn sharp right off roadbed
on a footpath that drops steeply from root clumps
to flat-top boulders by noisy North Fork of the
Wallace River — so pleasant a lunchsite many end
the hike here. For human goats and waterfall
fans, the trail across the rustic bridge climbs
steeply but easily 500 steps, then hits a rocky
slope with few handholds. Slowly, carefully does
it. Above, the trail levels in open forest, then
climbs again. Only 100 feet more to a tiny viewpoint by a big stump, with just a wire separating viewer from precipice. The cataract seems as
high as Snoqualmie Falls, but is broken, dropping
to various levels. Venture no farther. Loose rock
and hidden soft slopes add danger.

Old-timers full of memories worked for the
Gold Bar Logging Company and Wallace Falls
Timber Company in the area north of Wallace
River beginning 1916. The old trestle was built in
1921, says one old-timer. The railroad ran east
across the river below the falls, switched back
west, then east again to a point above the falls.
Scattered between trestle and clearing are more
remains of the logging kingdom.

Round trip 6 miles
Allow 4½ hours
High point 1120 feet
Elevation gain 880 feet
Best early spring or fall
Gravel road and dirt path

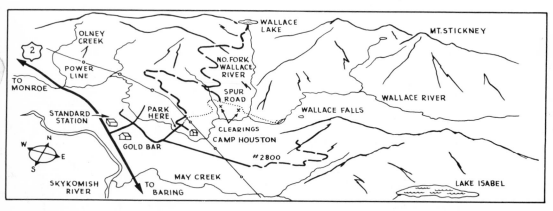

Heybrook Lookout, Mount Index, left Mount Persis, right

36   HEYBROOK LOOKOUT

Easy, pleasant, and among the most popular of Northwest mountain hikes. Though Heybrook Lookout is deeper in the hills than most trips in this book, the elevation is low and the route is open road with little wet brush to crowd, so the walk is enjoyable in early spring and early winter, even on rainy days. The road stays close to a Bonneville powerline, which our friend Mr. Bruin, whom we heard grunting from afar, had discovered made an open trail cross-country and naturally preferred to the road with its increasing human traffic. In early spring we encountered no less than a dozen hikers, along with another half-dozen of lazier breed on noisy motorbikes.

Columnar basalt near the top of Mount Pete

49   NORSE PEAK

Superlative view of Mt. Rainier from above the Crystal Mountain Ski Area in Snoqualmie National Forest. A good trail to the summit of Norse Peak, connecting with the Cascade Crest Trail for limitless rambling north or south.

Drive on US 410 to the side road to Crystal Mountain Ski Area (just south of Silver Spring summer houses), turn left 4 miles to large trail sign and parking lot on right. Walk up a logging road, left, 1/4 mile to trail. A spring by the road at trailhead is the last reliable water.

After a short, stiff climb, the tip of Rainier emerges over the ridge to the southwest. By 2 miles the entire summit can be seen and each upward step improves the picture.

The upper mile of trail may be confusing due to rebuilding: the new trail crosses the old in several places; take the one with the easier grade. Finding the peak is not difficult.

Norse Peak offers views north along the Cascade Crest as far as the Snoqualmie peaks, Mt. Daniel, and Mt. Stuart. Closer is Big Crow Basin, with good campsites. Directly across the valley, southwest, is the top of the skiers' chair lift, with Mt. Rainier as a massive backdrop, and also Mt. Adams farther south.

For campsites or water go north to the Cascade Crest Trail and Big Crow Basin, or go east and south, somewhat less than a mile, to trail shelter at beautiful Lake Basin, passing a meadow campsite beside a spring about halfway down.

Round trip 8 miles
Allow 6 hours
High point 6858 feet
Elevation gain 3750 feet
Best July through October
One day or backpack

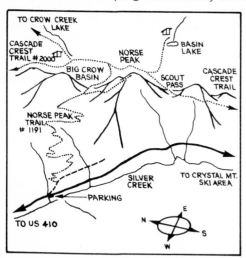

Crystal Mountain Ski Area from Norse Peak

50   SOURDOUGH GAP

Beginning in mile-high parkland, climb gently on well-maintained trail to extra-special views from the Cascade Divide on the edge of Mt. Rainier National Park.

Drive on US 410 to Chinook Pass. Park just east of pedestrian overpass at summit. A large map-signboard on the bank north above the highway shows the start of trail—the Cascade Crest Trail.

At 1½ miles is Sheep Lake, a tiny gem in the meadows. Good campsites. Immediately above the lake, at around 2½ miles, the trail reaches Sourdough Gap, a 6450-foot pass through a sharp ridge between the Rainier Fork of American River and Morse Creek. Broad views north and south from here, and in all directions if one climbs the 6743-foot summit forming the west wall of the pass.

If time and energy are available, continue north from Sourdough Gap. Along the Cascade Crest Trail ¼ mile is a junction with a trace trail left to Sheep Skull Gap, west and about 200 feet above the trail. An old trail, nearly invisible, enters Rainier National Park and descends from the gap through open country toward Crystal Lakes, in about ¼ mile reaching a point with an overlook of the lakes and a fine view of Rainier to the west. A one-way trip may be made by descending about a mile over open meadows, keeping to the right along the slopes, to the good campsites on the shore of Upper Crystal Lake.

A 3-mile trail goes down along Crystal Creek to intersect US 410 at a point 1.3 miles north of the White River entrance of Rainier National Park.

For another one-way trip, continue on the Crest Trail about 2 miles from Sourdough Gap and take the fork left up to Bear Gap and then down 2 miles to the Crystal Mountain Ski Area.

Round trip to Sourdough Gap 5 miles
Allow 4 hours
High point 6450 feet
Elevation gain 1021 feet
Best July through October
One day or backpack

Sheep Lake and Sourdough Gap

Magnificent viewpoint east of Rainier: into the dry Columbia Plateau of eastern Washington, over Bumping Lake to American Ridge, westward across the Cougar Lakes meadow-flats to Rainier and its satellites, southward over White Pass to the Goat Rocks and Adams.

Drive on US 410 to American River, take Bumping Lake road about 13.3 miles, then take left fork for about 1.6 miles. Just before reaching Copper Creek turn left up steep road marked "Mt. Aix Trail," drive a few yards and park. Rough road continues for ¼ mile; best to walk it. Clearly marked trail takes off from end. Fill canteens at creek within first ¼ mile.

The route is relentlessly uphill all the way, beginning with a traverse through deep forest nearly to a branch of Copper Creek, then switchbacking up and up a steep hillside. Rainier now emerges directly across the valley. At 2 miles the trail contours into subalpine meadows in the lower portion of a hanging valley, the source of the branch of Copper Creek. Continual switchbacks lead north away from the valley into open forest of whitebark pine, coming at 4 miles to a meadowy promontory that makes a good turnaround point. (Possible campsite in early summer when there is water.) Fine views of Rainier, Adams, and Goat Rocks.

From here the way leads south on a traversing ascent through arid-land meadows and scree slopes 2 miles to the crest of Nelson Ridge.

(Flowers climax in early July.) One can ramble in either direction along the broad, inviting crest, or contour 1 more mile to the summit of Mt. Aix, which once served as a fire lookout.

Lying on the east slope of the Cascades, Nelson Ridge receives less snow than the crest a few miles west; because of this, and the generally southwest exposures of the slope, the trail opens for travel much earlier, usually a full month, than trips on the divide north and south of Chinook Pass. However, the tread through the hanging valley may be snow-covered in June; if so, simply turn left out of the valley and climb through open forest to intersect the trail.

Round trip to Aix 14 miles
Allow 10 hours
High point 7772 feet
Elevation gain 3972 feet
Best mid-June to mid-August
One day

South along Nelson Ridge

An overview of an unusual plateau region splattered with scores of lakes, reached by a loop trip passing through an exceptionally large meadow close to the Cascade Crest.

Drive on US 410 to American River, take Bumping Lake road for 13.3 miles. At Y, take left fork (road #162) 6.2 miles to a side road and parking space, left, about ½ mile before end of road. Trail begins and ends here; take the left trail to start.

The trail climbs steadily through timber, crossing several streams on sturdy bridges. Just beyond the intersection with another trail, about 2 miles, are Blankenship Meadows, an extensive and level grassland, part of a 15-square-mile region of high plateau fantastically sprinkled with multitudinous lakes and ponds and puddles. A campsite lies under a clump of conifers near the east corner of the meadow; if streams are dry, a welcome find here will be the small marsh and spring up towards timber 100 yards east of the campsite.

Well out across the Meadows, and ascending the opposite side, the trail ends about 4 miles at a T with trail #1104, which goes left to Rimrock Lake and right to Twin Sisters Lakes. Take the right branch; at about ½ mile from the intersection, a trail leads sharply back to the left (south) 2½ miles to the fire lookout on Tumac Mountain. The top can also be reached from Blankenship Meadows by making a beeline to the higher slopes, on which the trail is easily found.

Although a longer loop can be made by continuing west down Tumac Mountain, the recommended one involves retracing the route to the last trail junction. Thence continue north, left, on trail #1104 again, to Twin Sisters Lakes, approximately 3 miles from Tumac Mountain. Certain camp spots at these very pretty lakes are popular, but privacy can be had at many less obvious locations. Meadows alternate with patches of forest. A good trail leads down from the lakes 2½ miles to the trailhead.

Round trip 12 miles
Allow 8 hours
High point 6340 feet
Elevation gain 2040 feet
Best mid-July through October
One day or backpack

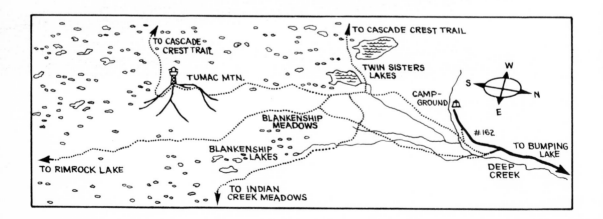

Blankenship Meadows

53   COUGAR LAKES

Summer-bright flowers carpet the meadows around two lovely lakes in the Bumping River region just east of Mt. Rainier National Park. In September the huckleberries ripen in profusion and the landscape glows with exceptional fall colors. From the ridge trails above Cougar Lakes, excellent views of Rainier to the west and of lesser mountains in all directions.

Drive on US 410 to American River, take Bumping Lake Road for about 13.3 miles. At Y, take right fork about 7 miles, cross Deep Creek, and continue along the south side of Bumping Lake to the end of the Upper Bumping Lake Road in Snoqualmie National Forest. The clearly marked trail, #970, leaves road's end.

At 1/3 mile a wide, shallow stretch of the Bumping River must be waded. Shortly beyond is an intersection with trails left and right along the river. Go straight ahead on a gradually ascending trail 4 miles through the forest to Swamp Lake shelter.

The two Cougar Lakes lie 2 miles farther. At a junction 1/2 mile beyond Swamp Lake's outlet, turn left onto the Cougar Lakes Trail, #958. Within 1/2 mile thereafter, keep left again, where one branch of the trail turns right to climb to the ridge crest. Pack horses use the trail a great deal, so it may be dusty or mucky; otherwise the hike is easy, through open meadows and alpine trees, with one glimpse of Mt. Rainier.

Little Cougar Lake, to the right from the trail, lies at the base of House Mountain, a wall of vertical rock just east of the Cascade Crest. A narrow isthmus separates the little lake from much larger Big Cougar Lake on the left. Many people camp on the lake shores, but the best sites are in the meadows above, where there is spring water, better views, and more space.

A trail just south of the upper end of Big Cougar goes up to the Cascade Crest Trail and splendid views from points north or south along the crest. A 5-mile loop side trip from a base at Cougar Lakes might be made by going north along the Cascade Crest Trail about 1½ miles to intersect Trail #958 and then hiking down it, back to Cougar Lakes.

Round trip to Cougar Lakes 14 miles
Allow 8 hours
High point 5100 feet
Elevation gain 1500 feet
Best August to mid-October
One day or backpack

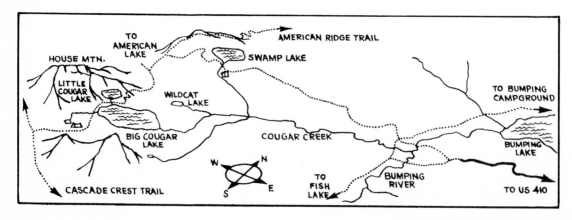

Cougar Lake and House Mountain

Easy ridge walk near timberline into splendid views. Farther on meadows slope to an attractive lake shaped like a Santa Claus boot.

Drive on State Highway 14 southeast of Rainier National Park to White Pass. Park at the lodge. Climb the nearby hill, expensively by chairlift or cheaply on foot; then follow a short trail to a junction with the Cascade Crest Trail.

For a longer and better walk, drive a mile east of White Pass to Leech Lake, where the Cascade Crest Trail intersects the highway. This alternative adds 5 miles and 1300 feet of elevation to the total trip but is much worthwhile.

South about a mile from the junction of the Cascade Crest Trail with the chair lift trail at a high pass in open alpine country, a striking view of Rainier dominates the horizon. Next the trail passes through a mountain basin at 5800 feet, brightened by little Miriam Lake. Needles and spires of volcanic rock punctuate the landscape. On the west, rising 900 feet above the basin, is Hogback Mountain. The trail climbs an arm of this mountain and at 3½ miles attains the highest elevation of the trip: a high, sharp ridge rimming a narrow basin. From here is a sweeping view of Goat Rocks with 12,202-foot Mt. Adams in the background.

Seen from the ridge, Shoe Lake appears blue-green, but after descending the 450 feet to the lakeshore, one finds the water crystal-clear. Excellent campsites at the lake. Wildflowers in profusion. Bear, deer, elk, and the ubiquitous marmot may be seen.

Round trip from lift 8 miles
Allow 5 hours
High point 6600 feet
Elevation gain 800 feet going, 466 feet returning
Best July 15 through October 15
One day or backpack

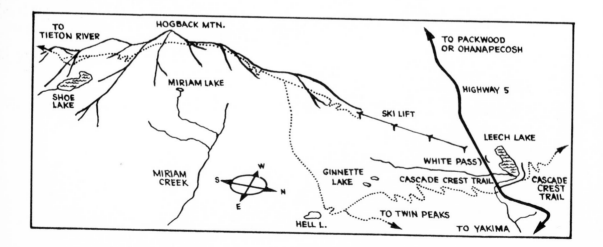

Shoe Lake

55   PACKWOOD LAKE

A quiet setting of heavily forested hills surrounding a big lake, with 7500-foot Johnson Peak dominating the scene. Other trails lead farther into the Goat Rocks Wilderness, where elk or goats may be sighted.

Drive to Packwood on State Highway 14; turn east at Packwood Ranger Station; drive about 6 miles to parking area, from which the trail starts. Entire trip is on public lands of Gifford Pinchot National Forest.

A very good trail, with no difficulties at all, climbs almost imperceptibly through mature forest with periodic views out over the Cowlitz Valley toward the Tatoosh Range and Mount Rainier. Several streams and springs, but only in the first 2 miles. Approaching the lake, the rugged Goat Rocks appear at its upper end. At the near end an intriguing small island stands well offshore. A Forest Service Guard Station is to the right of the trail; across the outlet stream and around the lake to the left is a well-developed campground. These and a rustic resort providing limited supplies, rental cabins and rowboats, are all that indicate civilization.

A walk to the flowered meadow at the head of the lake offers a look back across the water to Rainier. A loop trip of approximately 15 miles can be made from a trail junction near the campground into the Goat Rocks Wilderness to Packwood Saddle, returning via the Upper Lake Creek Trail.

Round trip 8½ miles
Allow 4 hours
High point 3150 feet
Elevation gain 350 feet
Best May through mid-November
One day or backpack

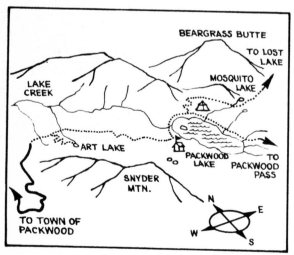

Packwood Lake and Johnson Peak on the right

56   SNOWGRASS FLAT

Continuous wide views from the rim of a huge alpine bowl in the Goat Rocks Wilderness. Loop trip, no retracing of steps.

Drive on State Highway 14 south from Packwood 2 miles. Turn left on Johnson Creek road #1302 and go 13 miles on this good gravel road. Turn left onto rocky road #1104, go 6 miles to Berry Patch parking area (½ mile before Chambers Lake). Plans for improved parking facilities may cause slight variations from these directions. At publication, trail #96 starts at Berry Patch and is prominently marked "Snowgrass Flat".

Dense evergreen forests characterize the first 4 miles of this circle trip. The return route can be seen rejoining trail #96 on the left ½ mile from the start. At 2 miles the bridge over Goat Creek has been tipped onto its side for some time, and the crossing is best made by side-stepping, facing in toward the structure. Two more creeks are crossed on footlogs. From Goat Creek to the 6500-foot level at 4½ miles the trail climbs somewhat abruptly. Within 3 hours from setting out, however, the good campsites at Snowgrass Flat are reached. Wonderful views from here. One can clearly see Mt. Adams to the south and Old Snowy and Ives Peak close above.

It is 3 miles farther, north along trail #86, to the next suitable campsites, at Goat Lake. The route is mostly level and completely in the open, on meadow slopes just below the ridge summit.

Expansive views are before the hiker all the time. He sees wildflowers at his feet, possibly mountain goats not far away, the trail ahead in a thin line skirting the edge of the great bowl-like cirque, and amazing mountains in the background. A side trip from Goat Lake west up a steep, rocky trail leads to Hawkeye Point, more than 7000 feet high.

Beyond Goat Lake, at 8 miles, the loop becomes trail #95, edging southerly around the bowl. The trail forks at 10½ miles and the hiker can select either branch. The left branch proceeds along the base of Goat Ridge to the junction with trail #96, and thence back to Berry Patch. The right branch makes a moderate ascent to unused Goat Ridge Lookout, then continues down to trail #95 and #96.

Because this exceptionally beautiful valley is so high, it holds snow well into summer and the steep slopes can be hazardous when snow-covered. Under such conditions a visit to Snowgrass Flat traveling trail #96 both directions is safer.

Total distance 13 miles
Allow 9 hours
High point 6700 feet
Elevation gain 2000 feet
Best July through September
One day or backpack

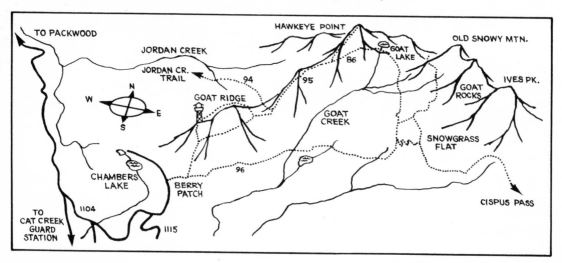

Snowgrass Flat and Mount Adams

57   ADAMS GLACIER CAMP

A moraine-and-meadow campsite at the 6000-foot level on Mt. Adams used as a base for summit ascents. The sunset and sunrise views from here—St. Helens and Rainier especially—are famous. Walk high onto the northwest ridge of Adams—to 8000 feet or more—without difficulty for increasingly broad views of volcanic terrain north and for a look down to Lava Glacier, or wander through moraines, snowfields, and creeks to the very foot of Adams Glacier.

Drive to Randle on State Highway 14. Turn south, crossing the Cowlitz River bridge. Follow the paved road, keeping to the left; after entering the Gifford Pinchot National Forest, continue on a gravel road (Forest Service #123) up the Cispus River to Adams Fork, 25 miles from Randle. Turn right onto road #106, keeping left after crossing the Cispus River bridge, for approximately 4½ miles. Turn right on road #101. At Midway Guard Station, turn right (south) and drive about 5 miles to Killen Creek Camp. Parking space is at the well-marked trail beginning ¼ mile farther on. Snow stays late on this high plateau; before July 4th be sure to check with the Forest Service Ranger at Randle to see if the trail and the road are open.

The trail climbs steadily at first, then gentles out. No water—until at 2 miles appears a most welcome meadow and stream. Here also a great view of the mountain, and a good campsite.

At 3½ miles Killen Creek trail joins the Cascade Crest Trail; an unimproved and sketchy climbers' trail continues southeast another 1½ miles to the high camp. During a late snowmelt or early winter the path may be hidden under snow patches and at best is none too easy to follow. However, the country is all open going. Simply be sure to keep to the right-hand slope at the crest of the ridge. The way trail peters out at a creek—and camp—on the south side of the ridge, a few yards from a saddle.

To avoid confusion on the return, be sure to look back from the ridge on the way in; mentally locate the end of the main trail and observe the terrain appearance.

The country surrounding the camp offers enough exploration opportunities to be worth staying several days. For an alternate return, go west (left) on the Cascade Crest Trail about ½ mile to the Divide Camp (Middle Fork Adams Creek) trail (#112), which rapidly descends 2 miles to a point on the road about 2 miles from the car.

Round trip 10 miles
Allow 7 hours
High point 6000 feet
Elevation gain 1500 feet
Best late June through October
One day or backpack

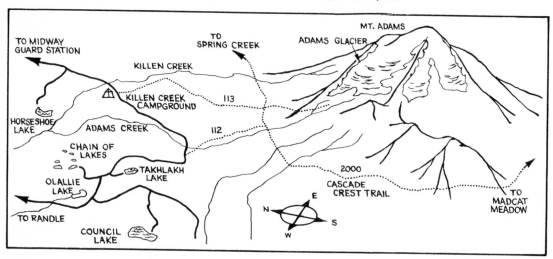

Mount Adams from Adams Glacier Camp

Memorable views of the graceful sweep of Mt. St. Helens, seemingly arm's-length from lesser peaks beyond Spirit Lake, and of Adams and Hood in the distance. The symmetrical white cone serenely reflected in the expanse of waters at its base seems little like a volcano active as recently as 1854. Trail trips can involve camping out a night or two, as along the 14-mile Mt. Margaret Loop, or walking a few hours and returning, as to Coldwater Lookout or Cedar Creek Camp.

Drive east from Castle Rock on State Highway 504 to Spirit Lake in Gifford Pinchot National Forest. Park at right side of road just before the bridge over the lake outlet (Toutle River). Well-marked trail takes off from left of road.

In early fall huckleberries may slow progress. Otherwise, travel is rapid over the $3\frac{1}{2}$ miles of gradually rising trail to St. Helens Lake. Here the narrow outlet stream, one of the sources of Spirit Lake, is crossed by a footlog, and not far beyond it the trail forks. The left fork, passing an agreeable lakeshore campsite, goes around the north end of the lake to Coldwater Lookout, 2 miles away. (Total distance from start, $5\frac{1}{2}$ miles.) The fine view from the lookout includes the two eye-catching lakes below. A walk of about 200 feet north on the peak gives a view towards Mt. Rainier.

The right fork goes to 5800-foot Mt. Margaret, overlooking Spirit Lake. In general the go-ing is good, though several steep places lend variety.

Beyond Mt. Margaret summit, which is 7 miles from the start, the trail snakes its way through Bear Pass, 9 miles (side trail, left, to campsites at small lakes of the Mt. Margaret backcountry, Grizzly Lake $\frac{1}{2}$ mile, and then through Norway Pass (side trail, left, to nearby Chicago Mine and to Meta Lake and beyond). Following a stream course out of the hills, the trail passes close to the Sweden Mine near the east end of Spirit Lake. A side trail, right, leads to lakeside Scout and YMCA camps.

Left along the shore is an improved campsite at Cedar Creek, 11 miles, where fireplaces, water, and sanitary facilities are provided. Since neither Cedar Creek Camp nor the next one, Donnybrook, are accessible by automobile, they are enjoyable destinations for short day or overnight hikes from Spirit Lake Campground.

Land in the Spirit Lake area is held in a checkerboard ownership pattern, therefore much of the route described here is over private land.

Total distance Mt. Margaret loop, 14 miles
Allow 2 days
High point 5858 feet
Elevation gain 2659 feet
Best July through September
One day or backpack

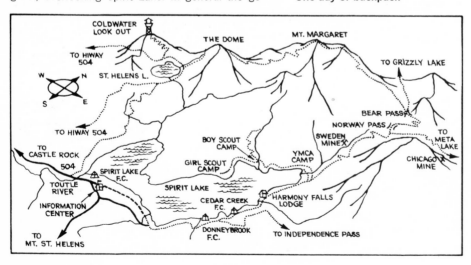

Mount St. Helens and Spirit Lake from the side of Mount Margaret

59   MT. PILCHUCK

Rising abruptly from Puget Sound lowlands, Pilchuck is one of the most prominent peaks on the Seattle skyline. The summit route is complicated by many side trails, and in places is too difficult for beginners to enjoy, but the superb view west over farms, towns, saltwaterways, and the Olympics and east and north into the Cascades is well worth the short but challenging climb.

Drive east from Granite Falls on Mountain Loop Highway about 11 miles, pass Verlot Ranger Station, turn right on Mt. Pilchuck Road. Drive to end of road and park in ski-area lot. Trail begins opposite lodge at foot of ski area. Drinking water is obtainable from snow runoff in early summer, but later in the year it is best to carry a canteen supply.

Although the trail is administered by the State Department of Natural Resources, it is a haphazard hodgepodge, for it receives no official maintenance. The trail begins to the right across the ski clearing. At the first fork go right, downhill, across a bridge. The trail soon becomes an uphill network of paths all of which lead to the same place. The main trail is marked with a letter "T" painted in yellow on trees and rocks. At the next fork, to the right is a switchback with a marker, to the left goes straight up. Take the left. Upon emerging from woods and returning to the ski hill, go under the chair lift and continue up to a yellow sign on a rock. It orders,

"Follow markers", and dabs of yellow paint (not orange) lead the way. The trail is quite rocky, possibly muddy, and there may be small snowfields until August. After a few switchbacks another fork is reached. Here one sign points ahead and seemingly down and reads, "½ mile to summit". The other points up the mountain and reads "¼ mile to summit—rocks—tough". Beginners and short-legged people (such as children) find this latter route difficult since it involves scrambling over large boulders. More experienced hikers enjoy the boulder-hopping. The longer route drops down at first, then switchbacks to the abandoned lookout atop the peak. Immediately below can be seen Frozen Lake, tucked in a snowfield pocket at the base of the summit cliffs.

In descending, the ski slope looks like a temptingly short way back to the road but it is rocky, brushy, marshy, garbage-cluttered, and generally poor going. It is wiser to stick with the trail. Many people have been perhaps not "lost", but certainly "confused" a day or two on Pilchuck; be watchful and avoid taking a turn which might mean going miles in the wrong direction.

Round trip 4 miles
Allow 5 hours
High point 5324 feet
Elevation gain 2124 feet
Best July through October
One day

Three Fingers Mountain from the side of Mount Pilchuck

60　MT. FORGOTTEN

A popular and rather easy trail following a curving, narrowing valley to its end, then ascending Mt. Forgotten to flower-filled meadows and wide views. Perry Creek Falls is worth a pause on the way.

Drive from Granite Falls on Mountain Loop Highway to 4 miles east of Silverton, turn left on Perry Creek logging road, go 1½ miles to end. Turn around, then park. Large sturdy sign marks start of trail toward the creek.

The upswept hillside to the right of the trail brings many small plants to eye-level; a great place for botanical study. Columbine, yellow violet, monkeyflower, bedstraw, maidenhair fern, licorice fern, parsley fern—all are presented to the alert observer. Other natural beauties, more likely to be noticed, are the cascades streaking the cliffy slopes of Stillaguamish Peak, left, and Mt. Dickerman, right. At 2 miles the trail edges Perry Creek Falls, where the water gathers in a smooth silent pool before sweeping through a rocky cleft to drop in a churning, roaring mass. A campsite here is too cramped to be anything but marginal. Only a short distance farther is a comfortable, improved campsite, with a bank of avalanche lilies nearby. Boulder-hop across the creek here, or, if early-season high waters make this impossible, search upstream for a better crossing.

The trail now has reached almost to the base of Twin Peaks, which block the head of the valley. It adopts a more northward direction and switchbacks up through the open woods on Mt. Forgotten. An avalanche clearing to the left off the trail is a mass of blueberries in season, and a good vantage point any time for restful contemplation of Big Four Mountain. The upper reaches of the trail cut through wide meadows of particularly lush flowers, in the midst of which the trail at length disappears. The summit is attainable by another mile of cross-country travel, and—keeping toward the right as the summit is approached—a scramble up rotten rock.

Round trip 8 miles
Allow 6 hours
High point 5500 feet
Elevation gain 3000 feet
Best June 15 through October
One day or backpack

White Chuck Valley and Glacier Peak from Mount Forgotten

61   MT. DICKERMAN

Strenuous, but worth it. On clear days hikers enjoy the mountain panorama all around; in late summer of good blueberry years they make slow progress through the enormous berry patch, a square half-mile in extent, near the top.

Drive east from Granite Falls on the Mountain Loop Highway. About 17½ miles east of Verlot Ranger Station (½ mile beyond Perry Creek) is an inconspicuous sign, "Mt. Dickerman Trail", on the left, and off-road parking space for five or six cars. The trail is honest—it starts uphill at once.

Switchbacks, switchbacks, all the way. But cool and peaceful through dense forest at first, with a smooth, springy surface underfoot. At 1½ miles is the first water, a small rivulet. Water reappears several times in the next mile, sometimes as pretty little cascades. At 2¼ miles a brook flows in the trail a short distance, and near here is a good campsite in a sheltered hollow with a western view. The blueberry bushes begin at this point, and stretch in unbroken masses along the way for a mile. In the midst of the meadow a side trail cuts downhill to a patch of trees, and an excellent campsite beside a small pond.

Beyond the plateau of berries the trail again switchbacks up the last, somewhat steeper, mile

to the summit, edging along thrilling dropoffs to the north (patches of snow usually visible at the bottom, no matter what the time of year). The very top is a patch of rock cropping out through thin soil, where the weary hiker can rest with feet dangling in air 200 feet above scree.

The view is all-directional. To the north across the basin of Perry Creek is Stillaguamish Peak and Mt. Forgotten. East is glittering Glacier Peak, some 15 miles away, and Sloan Peak, nearer. South and far below is tiny Barlow Point. Toward the west is Big Four Mountain and the valley of the South Fork Stillaguamish River. A glorious place to loiter over lunch.

Round trip 8 miles
Allow 7 hours
High point 5995 feet
Elevation gain 4000 feet
Best August and September
One day or backpack

Big Four Mountain from the side of Mount Dickerman

"Infinite riches in little room": Alaska cedars, old mines, interesting minerals, waterfalls, bench meadows, rock-basin ponds, lakes, and broad views of Monte Cristo peaks. Thanks to the steepness and poor condition of the trail, there are few hunters, few horses, and no scooters —great for walks in the hunting season. No fishermen, either, since Crater Lake is barren.

Drive east from Granite Falls on the Mountain Loop Highway toward Monte Cristo. East 2 miles from Barlow Pass cross the South Fork of the Sauk River and park on road shoulder ¼ mile beyond. Trail, possibly marked by tattered cardboard or wooden signs, begins on right side of road where an opening to river gravel appears.

Follow dry channel about 200 feet downstream, then turn left to the main river and a big footlog, flattened on top, which has been in place many years. The log terminates in a network of roots over a deep, slow pool—no place for the nervous or careless. (Children will need help.)

The trail, built by miners before the turn of the century, is not officially recognized and has had only casual maintenance by climbers since the miners left.

After a steep 1½ miles (1500 feet gained in the first mile), welcome water is reached where two streams pour through slot gorges beside an abandoned mine strewn with interesting artifacts. Entering alpine terrain, and sometimes obscured by vegetation, the trail traverses and climbs the valley wall above Weden Creek until, at 3 miles, it turns through a notch into the lower portion of Gothic Basin and ends in heather among glacier-polished-and-scratched buttresses. A fine campsite at the basin entrance; a better one a short way up-basin beside a shallow pond, on patches of heather amid convenient kitchen boulders.

Wander freely in all directions. Mines and prospect holes to investigate in the lower basin. Many specimens for the mineral-hunter in this contact zone between igneous and sedimentary rocks. Climb another 300 feet or so to reach Crater Lake, in a large cirque with Del Campo Peak on one side and Gothic on the other. Superb views from passes or ridges above the lake: across Weden Creek to Silvertip and all the peaks of the Monte Cristo group; down into the upper Sultan basin; over the Sauk to Sloan Peak. A select campsite is located on the ridge leading to Del Campo.

Round trip 6 miles
Allow 7 hours
High point 5000 feet
Elevation gain 2700 feet
Best August through October
One day or backpack

Rocks in Gothic Basin scratched and polished by glaciers

Sheep Gap Mountain from a small lake in Gothic Basin

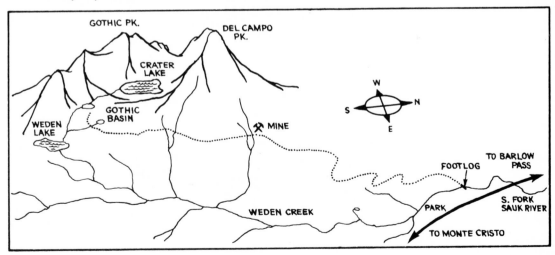

63   POODLE DOG PASS

From Monte Cristo, an old mining town of the 1890s, a rugged trail climbs to snow-fed Silver Lake at the base of Silvertip Peak. A popular camping spot despite the rough, steep approach.

Drive east from Granite Falls on the Mountain Loop Highway to Monte Cristo, now a privately owned resort. Park in the resort (for a fee) or outside (no cost) and walk a quarter-mile or so to the trail. (The public has an established right of foot travel across the private land.) At a pair of cabins below Monte Cristo Inn enter a road-like clearing marked by a Forest Service sign, "Silver Lake". Watch closely in 500 feet for a little sign, "trail", which points to the right. The resort management has marked the trail with pink plastic strips tied to trees.

Brush edges the trail for a long way at first and, if not recently trimmed, drenches travelers in wet weather. There are many slippery spots and several steep stretches where the hiker must clamber up ladderways of tree roots. Switchbacks are few and gullies many. All in all, a steady climb on a poor trail, but short.

National Forest land is entered at ½ mile. In 1 more mile is Poodle Dog Pass (indicated by a trail marker) and also a junction with a trail left to Twin Lakes. Enjoy a rewarding view from here of Wilmon Spires, then descend into a basin on the last ½ mile of trail. Silver Lake affords good campsites near the outlet, the only level space in the basin. To the west is 6100-foot Silvertip Peak; a permanent snowfield at its base extends all across that shore, providing a steady source of clear, cold water. Sometimes even in July the lake is still mostly ice-covered. By the end of summer blueberries abound.

From the lake one can see some of the mountains around Monte Cristo; for a better view, cross the outlet and climb on a trace of a trail partway up the ridge of Silvertip. In about half an hour stop and look back. (At prospect holes on the ridge are excellent specimens of mixed sulfide ores.)

Round trip 4 miles
Allow 3½ hours
High point 4500 feet
Elevation gain 1500 feet
Best July through October
One day or backpack

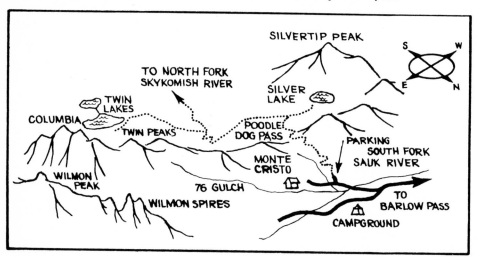

Silver Lake and Silvertip Peak from a hill above Poodle Dog Pass

64 GLACIER BASIN

A short scramble on an old miners' trail to meadows shut away from the outer world by walls of rock and snow. Mining relics abound. Also climbers.

Drive east from Granite Falls on Mountain Loop Highway to the entrance to Monte Cristo Resort. Continue to the left uphill to a campground, and as far beyond as the road is passable. Park wherever seems best; the 1½ miles past the campground have some rugged driving. The trail, unmarked, takes off from road's end. Logging activity may obliterate the beginning; keep in mind that the route lies close to Glacier Creek at all times.

A bit of moderate, then steep, uphill going leads to a waterfall (visible from road) which can be conveniently viewed from a nearby rock outcrop. A grim but short struggle follows, requiring much use of alder handholds to maintain footing—slow and slippery, but not hazardous. Above this unpleasantness the way levels out into a little talus-and-marmot-filled valley which cuts through the barrier ridge that gives Glacier Basin its sense of seclusion. At the tailings of an old mine the trail fades away. One can follow the creek into the basin—on easy snow in early summer, through a muddle of brush, grass, and boulders in late summer. Alternatively, go a few yards beyond the tailings and find an easy way to climb about 50 feet on dirt and boulders to a flat causeway carrying a large rusty pipe. This causeway-trail leads into the basin.

The barrier ridge keeps the secret of the basin to the last minute. Then, abruptly turning a corner, one sees creeks meandering through flat meadows, sandy-shored ponds, flowers, dippers, grass, waterfalls, big boulders, snowfields, and all sorts of fun. Many superb campsites at and near the basin entrance. At the head of the basin, atop a knoll named for climber Ray Rigg, is another campsite offering more privacy and a broader view. Higher up is easy scree and a gully leading to an upper cirque with glaciers, moraines, and waterfalls; experienced hikers equipped with ice axes can walk to the col between Monte Cristo and Wilmon Peaks, overlooking Columbia Glacier and Lake Blanca.

The road to Monte Cristo Resort is usually plowed out by early June but the basin is normally snow-filled until July. One should be aware that although the trail is in Mt. Baker National Forest, it is not officially recognized, is not maintained except by occasional climbers' work parties, and is pretty much the way it grew in early mining days.

Round trip from road end 2 miles
Allow 3 hours
High point 5000 feet
Elevation gain from road end 1000 feet
Best July through October
One day or backpack

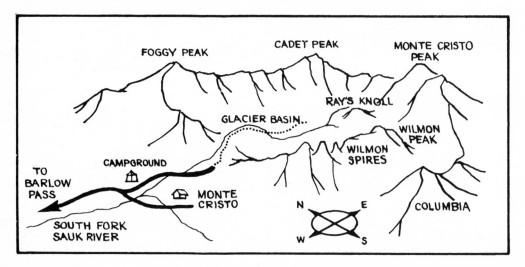

Glacier Basin and Monte Cristo Peak

65   MEADOW MOUNTAIN

A long rolling parkland ridge with views down to forests of the White Chuck and east to the ice of Glacier Peak.

Drive from Darrington on the Mountain Loop Highway 10½ miles, cross the White Chuck River and turn left onto the White Chuck River Road. Go about 6 miles to a river crossing and take Crystal Road #327, the first road to the left after the bridge. Several spurs branch off but the main track (Meadow Mountain Road #3128) is well-marked with signs pointing to Meadow Mountain.

The Forest Service has a temporary sign at the beginning of the trail, but it is often destroyed by logging operations and road construction (to be completed 1967) underway in the vicinity. Be sure to park far enough off the road to allow large trucks to pass.

The trail climbs steadily through subalpine forest, breaking into open meadows at about 1½ miles. A fine creek here and a small campsite upstream ¼ mile. A wonderful view from the ridge directly above the trail; a much better one in another 1½ miles, where the trail rounds a turn in the ridge and comes face to face with Glacier Peak and the full depth of the White Chuck valley. This is a good turnaround point for the day's hike.

Backpackers may adventure farther, following the trail as far as time permits. Meadow Mountain joins the equally long ridge of Fire Mountain, which in turn joins Glacier Peak. The ridges are inviting, dotted with alpine trees and flower fields. A campsite providing both good space and constant water is reached in a basin about 4 miles. Equally fine camping is available at Diamond Lake, reached by a side trail from ridge crest another mile farther, or at less-frequented Emerald Lake cross-country northwest over a heathered rise from the outlet of Diamond Lake.

Round trip 5 miles
Allow 4 hours
High point 5400 feet
Elevation gain 1550 feet
Best July through October
One day or backpack

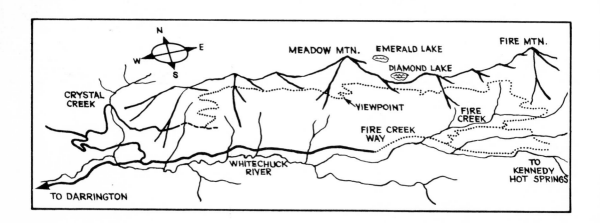

White Chuck Valley and Glacier Peak from the Meadow Mountain Trail

66   KENNEDY RIDGE AND HOT SPRINGS

Glacial ice and volcanic heat—personal contact with both on a single expedition, plus a close view of Glacier Peak.

Drive on State Highway 530 to Darrington, take Mountain Loop Highway 10½ miles. At the White Chuck River road turn left and drive to end at picnic spot parking area. Trail begins here, clearly marked "White Chuck River Trail, Kennedy Hot Springs."

A new trail provides easy traveling, at times right beside the rushing White Chuck, with glimpses of Glacier Peak up the valley. Just beyond Fire Creek the Old White Chuck trail (now marked "Fire Creek Way") and the new trail separate. The new route follows benchland then drops to cross Pumice Creek at 2 miles (note spectacular cliffs of tuff). The trail then follows near the river and joins the old route again at Glacier Creek, 4.5 miles. A gentle ½ mile ascent brings one to the flats at Kennedy Creek and the 5-mile sign where Kennedy Ridge trail takes off to the left. A little more than ¼ mile farther on, across Kennedy Creek, are Kennedy Hot Spring, a Forest Service guard station, two shelters, and a few tent spots.

The principal hot spring is across a wooden bridge by the guard station, then left about 100 feet upriver. A blissful bath awaits the tired hiker who does not scorn the simple accoutrements: a rustic shed for dressing and a wooden coping around a concrete slab pool (capacity: 4).

To make personal acquaintance of glaciers, take the Kennedy Ridge trail, very steep at first, then steadily uphill for a mile along an old forested moraine from which ice can be glimpsed through the trees. Intersect and join the Cascade Crest Trail and climb yet another mile, first up short switchbacks through red and gray andesite lava, then along the heathery moraine crest to where the trail turns left to cross Glacier Creek a few yards away (good campsite). Leave the trail and continue up the open-forested crest of the old moraine, abruptly emerging onto a new and barren moraine deposited by the Kennedy Glacier.

Memorable scenes, these: glaciers streaming from the summit of the silent volcano; green meadows; wasteland of the "valley train" below; White Chuck forests extending westward. The energetic can boulder-hop and stream-leap right up to the ice snout.

An alternative return route for those not dismayed by disappearing tread and countless blow-downs is the unmaintained Glacier Ridge Trail, ½ mile north from Glacier Creek, offering diversified scenes on the way back to the White Chuck River.

Round trip to Kennedy Ridge 18 miles
Allow 2 or 3 days
High point 6100 feet
Elevation gain 3800 feet
Best August and September
Backpack

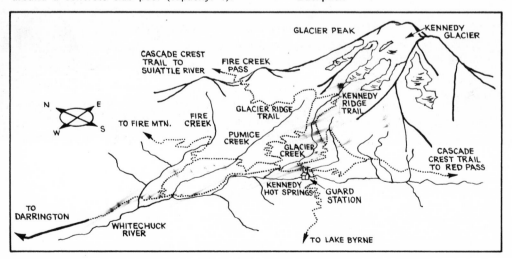

Glacier Peak from Kennedy Ridge Trail

67   MT. PUGH

Big views of Sloan, Glacier, Shuksan, Baker, and many other peaks from the dry, rocky summit ridge. Energetic hikers can reach the very top by scrambling. Abundant wildlife.

Drive on the Mountain Loop Highway along the South Fork of the Sauk River (14 miles from Darrington, 10 miles from Barlow Pass). Turn east on the Mt. Pugh road, #3131, a logging road, and go about a mile. The trail sign is just above the second hairpin turn. Park off the road at the turn, or along the road below.

One could almost walk barefoot along the first 3 miles, so springy is the needle-carpeted forest trail. Canteens can be filled at two streams crossed near the beginning of the hike, but really excellent water is available ½ mile along at Deer Springs, 100 feet below what appears to be the outlet of Metan Lake. The lake, at 1½ mile, has no visible outlet or inlet. From here the trail climbs steeply, with many switchbacks, up forested slopes to timberline at 3 miles. Then it continues in the open, traversing rockslide where the trail is poor. The route is easy to see on the way up, but be sure to observe landmarks where the trail leaves timberline so that it can be found on the return. At 3¾ miles is Stujack Pass, a sharp notch, with permanent snowfields on the far side. Leisurely or inexperienced hikers make this their turnaround point.

Even strong walkers may require 1½ hours more to reach the summit. This upper part of the trail, abandoned and dangerous, weaves in and out along a knife-edge ridge where strict attention is necessary to avoid accidents. Tripods in place above the pass and just below the summit were used to hand-crank lumber up the hill for building the Forest Service lookout which once was on the peak. There are three extremely steep pitches above the first tripod; the footing is good, but avoid knocking loose rocks down on people below. The trail grows narrower and less distinct and gradually becomes climbing, requiring hands as well as feet in the steeper places.

Angular rock is a noticeable feature of Mt. Pugh. Look for "Goat Bridge", a plug 5 to 8 feet wide, 80 feet long, in a cleft of the ridge south of the summit. Watch also for goats, deer, bear, marmots, conies—and salamanders.

A suggested campsite is at timberline on the edge of the meadows, but water supply may be a problem late in the season. The trail is open to timberline by July; dangerous snowpatches above that persist until August.

Round trip 11 miles
Allow 8 hours
High point 7224 feet
Elevation gain 5600 feet
Best August and September
One day or backpack

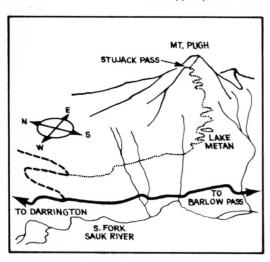

Mount Pugh from Meadow Mountain

An alpine lake suitable for camping, swimming, fishing, rafting, and looking up to cliffs and ice of Cadet and Foggy Peaks. Remains of old mine buildings can still be found; the U.S. Geological Survey map of 1899 shows six structures clustered at the outlet. In those days a wide wagon road led to the lake; its cedar planking is still used by the trail in places.

Until recently the trail began at the Sauk and followed the entire length of the ancient wagon road; now much of the dense valley forest and the historic road have been destroyed by timber sales which led to wind-throws, out-of-control slash fires, and salvage logging.

To reach the start of what trail is left, drive on the Mountain Loop Highway east from Granite Falls to Barlow Pass, then north about 4 miles toward Darrington. Turn right onto Elliott Creek logging road, somewhat north of Elliott Creek. Go 3 miles to a marked parking space. **Be warned: park there; do not block the road!** Hike beyond the parking area along the lower fork of the logging road. Trail begins 10 feet past the sign, "Goat Lake Trail."

Evidences of the early mining efforts remain along the trail. The wheel of an ore cart rests under ferns beside a stream crossing. A steep-roofed miners' cabin is half-hidden by a thicket.

The trail ascends very gradually for the first 1½ miles, then becomes fairly steep and switchbacks repeatedly. The original road crossed Elliott Creek at the beginning of this steep part, but the present-day foot trail does not. Hikers should not mistake a rocky gully going to the left away from the stream for the correct path. The more comfortable footing of the real trail leads on up another ¼ mile; the wagon road then rejoins it from the right, and the route soon approaches the lake.

The outlet stream is at the right. Ruined foundations in a clearing near the remains of a dam indicate much activity in years gone by. One can reach a secluded campsite on the high opposite bank by skipping nimbly across the disappearing pilings. The trail continues left along the lake shore, passing many campsites amid the trees. Beyond a rocky point the trail becomes progressively poorer and disappears. In early summer a stream laces the steep rock with a delicate, spreading cascade. Its waters course the level floor of the promontory and tumble into the cold transparent lake below. The blossoms of shooting star and false Solomon's seal nod in the spray.

Round trip 4 miles
Allow 3 hours
High point 3162 feet
Elevation gain 660 feet
Best June through October
One day or backpack

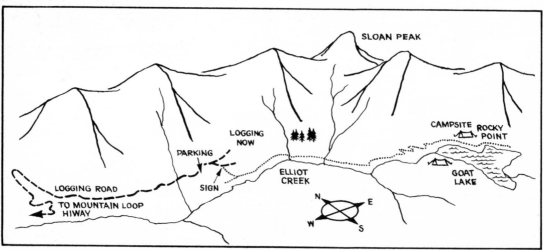

Goat Lake and cliffs below Foggy Peak

69   IMAGE LAKE

Possibly more photographs have been taken here than from any other point in the Glacier Peak Wilderness, and with good reason. The view of Glacier Peak across the Suiattle forests, its image reflected in the meadow-surrounded lake, is a climax in the memories of any North Cascades traveler.

Drive to the Suiattle River Road, reached through Darrington on State Highway 530 or through Rockport on State Highway 20. Continue to the very end (the last mile is rough) to ample parking area. The well-marked trail starts from the upper section of the terminal loop road. Avoid the more easily found trail at river-edge, which leads in a few yards to a splendid picnic spot on sand-and-gravel bars.

The trail, which enters Glacier Peak Wilderness at 1½ miles, follows close to the Suiattle River for 5 rather muddy miles, through deep forest (including a section of rain forest near the road) to a shelter at Canyon Creek, then 3 miles more, climbing away from the river to a trail fork. Here it leaves the Suiattle River Trail and begins the ascent of Miner's Ridge, passing the last water for 3 steep miles about ½ mile from the junction. After climbing through gradually opening forest, at 10 miles the trail affords spectacular views. At 11 miles the trail again branches left (water a few hundred yards downtrail) and ascends very steeply over 2 miles of incessant switchbacks to the open ridge crest at 13 miles. By now the scenery is glorious. A short spur trail left leads to Miner's Ridge Lookout; Image Lake, and to Kennecott's mining activities ½ mile farther.

Image Lake has become so famous in recent years that the area around the shelter, and the entire shore, is usually crowded in good weather. Better and more private campsites are available throughout the lake basin; for even greater privacy walk about ½ mile to the obvious low saddle above the basin and drop down the north slope on the poorly-marked Canyon Lake Trail to any of several nice off-trail hollows.

Other side trips from the lake include a short meadow hike north (left) to a little knoll offering good views of Canyon Creek and Lake; a longer off-trail walk east (right) along the crest of Miner's Ridge toward the 7870-foot summit of Plummer Mountain; and a trail walk east to Lady Camp in a small cirque 1½ miles from Image Lake, and to Kennecott's mining activities ½ mile farther.

Round trip 28 miles
Allow 2 to 4 days
High point 6050 feet
Elevation gain 4400 feet
Best late July through October
Backpack

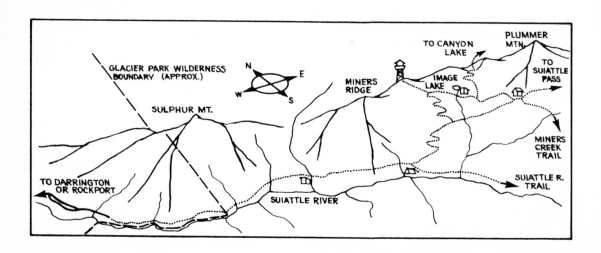

Glacier Peak from Image Lake, a 20-minute walk from Kennecott's proposed giant open-pit copper mine

A cross-mountain traverse of the Glacier Peak Wilderness from Puget Sound country to the Columbia valley. Follow the forested Suiattle River valley, climb to the high meadows of Miner's Ridge, cross Suiattle and Cloudy Passes, descend to the lakes of Lyman Basin, and continue out Railroad Creek to Lake Chelan.

Approach as for Image Lake, described elsewhere. The hike can also be made in the reverse direction, starting from the east; in this case journey up Lake Chelan as described for Park Creek Pass, leaving the ferry at Lucerne two-thirds of the way up-lake.

From a westside starting point, follow the first 8 miles of the Suiattle River Trail to the junction with the Cascade Crest Trail, at which point take the left branch, ascending Miner's Ridge with gentle switchbacks, contouring east past the Image Lake Trail, left, at 11 miles. (Include Image Lake in the itinerary by making a side trip here, returning to the Suiattle Pass Trail by way of Glacier Peak Mines.) Just past this junction the trail crosses the creek from Image Lake and climbs through small trees and across a hot and dusty hillside to the eastern end of the Image Lake Trail. Here are two mining company shacks.

The trail beyond this point comes out above timberline and makes its way through meadows and past more debris of the Glacier Peak Mines toward Suiattle Pass, 15½ miles, where to the right of the trail in a small flat meadow is a nice camp spot. After descending a short distance to cross the South Fork Agnes Creek, where the Cascade Crest Trail forks left, the trail climbs to 6438-foot Cloudy Pass, 17½ miles.

The route, now the Railroad Creek Trail, continues to good camping on the west shore of Lyman Lake, 18 miles. A steep way trail climbs about 500 feet to Upper Lyman Lake, from where the Lyman Glacier is an easy stroll. The outlet of Lyman Lake spreads in unusual fashion over smooth slabs of granite, becoming Railroad Creek, which 3 miles below tumbles over the Crown Point Falls. Hart Lake, reached after a 1500-foot drop, is about 24 miles from the start.

The last 3½ miles of the transmountain trek lead into a faint jeep track which guides to the ball park at Holden Village, an abandoned mining town now operated as a summer center for Lutheran church activities. For the rather expensive taxi service from Holden over the dusty road 12 miles to the dock at Lucerne, arrangements must be made well in advance by writing the Lucerne Resort, Chelan, Washington.

Total distance 27½ miles
Allow 5 to 7 days
High point 6438 feet
Elevation gain 4778 feet
Best July and August
Backpack

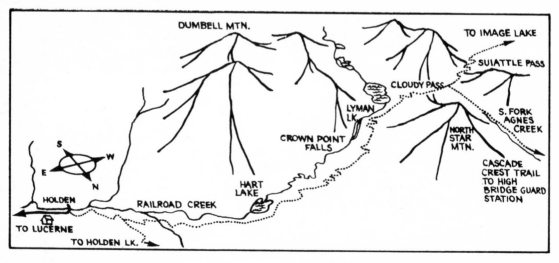

Lyman Lake and North Star Mountain

71   BUCK CREEK PASS

One of the richest flower gardens of the Cascades—greenery and color in all directions—but also noted for the unusually fine views of Glacier Peak's largest and longest glaciers across the broad valley of the Suiattle River. Can be a transmountain backpack expedition either to Image Lake and Suiattle River Road or to Lyman Basin and Lake Chelan, or a weekend backpack visit to Buck Creek Pass, or merely a one-day hike up the trail a ways.

Drive on US 2 to Coles Corner 18 miles east of Stevens Pass, turn north on State Highway 207 for 5 miles, then right 5 miles on State Highway 209 to just east of Chiwawa River crossing; or from Leavenworth drive north on State Highway 209 to just east of river crossing. Go north on narrow, gravel, Chiwawa River Road 24 miles to informal parking spaces at Phelps Creek.

Route begins by crossing Phelps Creek bridge (go around gate), passes on old road through inoperative mining town of Trinity, past two large fuel tanks on the left. A few yards beyond Forest Service "Buck Creek Trail" sign, take right fork. Next appears a sign announcing entrance to Glacier Peak Wilderness, at a creek and a dismantled bridge; from here the road goes up a steady grade to the 1-mile marker. A few hundred yards beyond marker, a footpath turns left from the road; travel thereafter is more pleasant and the route easier to follow.

The trail goes along the Chiwawa River for 2½ miles, crosses it on a broad bridge, then enters the valley of Buck Creek and climbs up two valley steps. Just beyond the 4-mile marker the trail traverses an avalanche meadow. Here are impressive views of the black north face and hanging ice of Buck Mountain. For a one-day walk, this makes a logical turnaround.

At 6, 6½, and 7 miles the trail crosses Buck Creek by fords or footlogs, as the hiker may prefer. The first of these crossings constitutes the next short-trip turnaround point, in a meadow below eight waterfalls coursing down from an upper cirque. Beyond the third crossing the last 1½ miles of trail mounts very steeply uphill almost to the pass. The approach to the pass is confused by bewildering side trails to camp spots and along old sheep routes. At an unmarked fork ¼ mile before the pass summit, the left branch goes up to a camp; the right jogs downhill to the 8-mile marker, the creek, and then up to the pass and a profusion of signs. Campsites abound, here and all along the trail. Explorations from the pass also abound; one of the most dazzling being to the aptly-named Flower Dome.

Round trip 17 miles
Allow 2 or 3 days
High point 6000 feet
Elevation gain 3028 feet
Best in August and September
One day or backpack

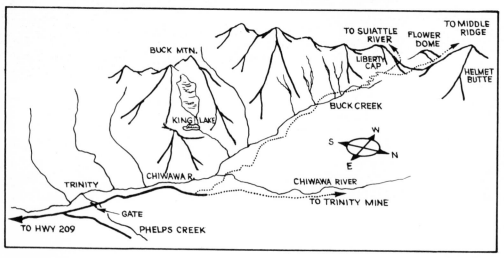

Glacier Peak from Buck Creek Pass

72   ENTIAT MEADOWS

The source of the Entiat River high in the Glacier Peak Wilderness is reached by a long but almost level trail. Campsites in flower-dotted Entiat Meadows at trail-end have wide views of the hanging glacier on Mt. Maude. A sunny rainshadow approach to the wild Cascades.

Drive north from Wenatchee on US 97 to Entiat, then left on Entiat River Road. Trail takes off from large parking area at end of road.

The wide, dusty trail ascends through dry, open forest. At 4 miles the Cow Creek Meadows trail goes left, and ½ mile from the river passes a fisherman-crowded campsite and scooter parking lot in the woods surrounding Myrtle Lake. At 5 miles another side trail left leads steeply through an old burn to Larch Lakes, with a shelter and ample meadow camping space. Excellent campsites, one cool and shady, one open to the sun, can be found where Snow Brushy Creek joins the Entiat and a mile farther on just before the next junction. The main trail begins to climb more perceptibly, through denser forest, and at 8 miles enters the Glacier Peak Wilderness.

At 8½ miles is the trail to Ice Lakes, an excellent alternate destination. The very fine Ice Creek Shelter is located a few hundred feet up the trail; additional camp spots abound. The last mile of the 7-mile hike from the Entiat River is cross-country, but the lakes are easy to find. Although the valley is surrounded by cliffs, there is a steep, grassy hillside at the head of the valley.

The lakes lie just over the top and to the left.

The Entiat River Trail continues several miles past Ice Lakes Trail before reaching the broad valley of Entiat Meadows, once over-grazed by sheep and still deeply rutted. Camping possibilities without number in the 4½ miles of meadows. The whole panorama of the gigantic cirque is fully visible, with Mt. Fernow, Seven-fingered Jack, and Mt. Maude, each over 9000 feet, providing the high points. Also of interest are the retreating remnants of the Entiat Glacier.

Experienced hikers may vary the return by taking the Larch Lakes or Cow Creek Meadows Trails to a trail along the ridge crest of the Entiat Mountains, crossing Fifth of July, Rampart, and Garland Mountains, and descending Shetipo Creek to the starting point. This alternative is more difficult and less well-marked than the Entiat River Trail, but is one of the best high-country walks in the Cascades.

Round trip 30 miles or more
Allow 4 days or more
High point 5500 feet
Elevation gain 2400 feet
Best July through October
Backpack

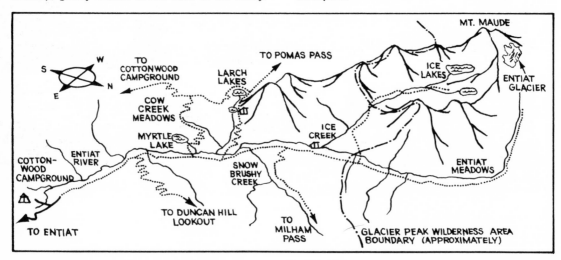

Ice Creek Falls

73   PARK CREEK PASS

A long and somewhat complicated journey is required to see at close hand these giant glaciers and enormous peaks, mountains so splendid they have been called "The Switzerland of America". Three peaks rise above 9000 feet, helping form the highest part of the Cascade Crest, with the Park-Stehekin-Chelan drainage into the Columbia on one side and the Thunder-Skagit drainage into Puget Sound on the other. An effort must be made to reach this country—and therefore it is still wild—yet the hike to Park Creek Pass is not really difficult at all.

Drive on US 97 north from Wenatchee to about 9 miles north of Entiat. Turn left on paved secondary road to Lake Chelan State Park, turn left at the park and parallel the lake to the end of the road at Twenty-five Mile Creek. Plan to board the **Lady of the Lake** at the dock at 10 A.M. daily during the summer, on its 50-mile journey up one of the most remarkable lakes in the world, the flooded channel of an ancient glacier.

The voyage is reminiscent of similar ones elsewhere: along the German Rhine past Bonn, Andernach, and Koblenz, or up the Hudson River from New York to Albany, or on Sweden's canal system to Stockholm, or from village to village around Lake Constance. All offer restful boat travel through avenues of changing beauty typifying the local economy. Lake Chelan is equally worthy of broad fame. Along its shores are orchards, resorts, state parks, national forests, and logging operations. Dry, rolling hills form the shoreline at the southern end of the lake, northward giving way gradually to high mountains. One looks up and up to 8000-foot peaks rising from the water's edge, and can imagine how their steepness extends down into the lake, 1500 feet deep in places.

Nearing the resort town of Stehekin one can see Booker and Buckner Mountains, which rise above Park Creek Pass, the ultimate destination. To travel the last miles up the Stehekin River road, make arrangements at the dock to rent a car; or hire a ride, with later pick-up at a specified hour and day. The cost is considerable for one pocketbook—though not unreasonable—and is best shared among several people. Drive or ride 20 miles along the unpaved, almost carless Stehekin road.

Park Creek trail leaves the road about 2½ miles past Bridge Creek, marked by a sign. The first 2 miles are rather steep; beyond a small campsite at a footlog crossing of the stream the grade becomes easier. The trail lies in heavy forest, with only occasional glimpses of the very high country on all sides. Those who start hiking the same day they come up the lake can't get on the trail until about 3 P.M., so slow-paced hikers will

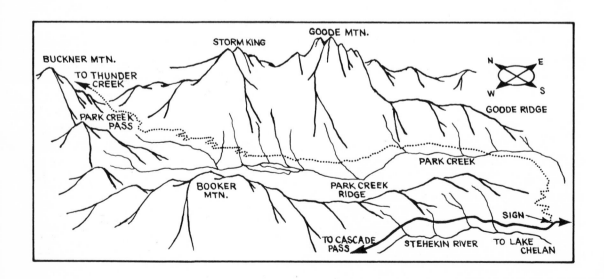

want to camp along the lower trail. There are several campsites, small but adequate.

At about 4½ miles a sign points right, to Mt. Goode, but there is no trail, simply a cross-country route used by climbers attempting the 9300-foot peak. Hikers continue straight ahead, and up, ascending a steep, long step in the valley which brings them out of forests and into parkland. At the top of the step the grade flattens out somewhat and the summit of the pass comes in sight. The meadows, streams, and pine trees here make a great place to camp, dominated by Booker's giant north wall, and by Buckner and Goode.

The top of the pass is a gentle climb from the meadows into rocks and year-round snow. For a superb side trip, go west from the pass about ½ mile, to where the terrain drops down, then contour north through easy meadows and moraines to a stupendous view of the 2-mile expanse of Boston Glacier.

For an extended trip which avoids retracing steps, go through the pass and down the north slope along Thunder Creek, all the way to Diablo, about 2 days' backpack travel. (See description.) Such a journey would necessitate planning beforehand to have transportation waiting at Colonial Creek Campground on Ross Lake. Or the hiker can return the way he has come.

Round trip to pass 15.8 miles
Allow an afternoon and following morning
High point 6400 feet
Elevation gain 4100 feet
Best July 15 through September 15
Backpack

Air view of Park Creek Pass, Mount Buckner (left) and Mount Logan (right).

74 GRASSHOPPER PASS

Big sky country with easy-roaming ridges, massive peaks, and deep valleys. Though precisely on the Cascade Crest, the miles of mountains west soak up most of the rain; clumps of pine and larch and patches of delicate dryland meadows thrive on relatively sunny slopes. On a good day one can walk forever.

Drive on Highway 20 up the Methow Valley 14 miles beyond Winthrop; turn right on County Road #23, pass Mazama (post office) at 1/2 mile. Pavement ends in 2 1/2 miles; continue on gravel road 17 miles to Harts Pass. Turn left on Brown Bear road #3739, drive 2 miles south (passing extensive new campground) to end.

The Cascade Crest Trail hereabouts is being relocated to bring it as much as possible out of valleys into high country; perhaps by 1969 the new route will be open south to Rainy Pass. This segment, though actually complete (1967) beyond Granite pass, is signed "Glacier Pass." The way ascends gently around a valley head, a mine above and mining trash in grass below, to the east shoulder of 7433-foot Tatie Peak, then up and down across the face of Tatie to a saddle south, and along the ridge crest with good looks right into Ninety-nine Canyon. A traverse over the scree of a no-name peak leads to another saddle, this one with a picture of 8450-foot Ballard. Down east are forests and valley-bottom meadows of Trout Creek, draining to the Methow.

Switchbacks drop several hundred feet into a bouldery basin at 4 miles, and a natural camp. The only dependable late-summer water on the

way, in a small cold creek springing from mossy rocks and flowing through heather and flowers, is framed by wispy larches.

The trail climbs some on the last mile to (approximately) 7100-foot Grasshopper Pass, a wide meadowy swale. Snowmelt water and thus grand camping in early summer. The trail continues up along the crest a quarter-mile before zig-zagging down and down 1500 feet to Glacier Pass, but Grasshopper has the full view of 8440-foot Azurite Peak and makes the logical turn-around.

Every slope and peak invites a side trip to inspect close-up the larches and pines and spruces, the blossoms on scree and buttress, and the colorful shales, slates, conglomerates, and sandstones with interesting igneous intrusions.

With a bit of extra ambition one can vary the trip by not using the trail at all, touching it at only one point between the road and Grasshopper— walking and scramb'ing up and down the crest the entire way. In fact, this is the best hiking route in very early summer, when steep snow blocks the trail but the sunny summits are covered with flowers.

Round trip 10 miles
Allow 8 hours
High point 7100 feet
Elevation gain 1200 feet
Best July through October
One day or backpack

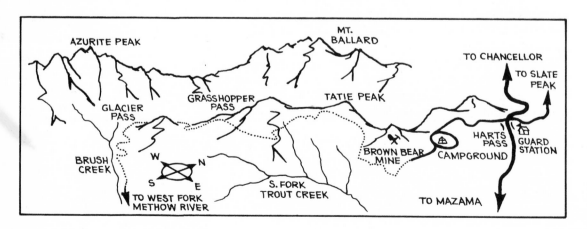

Air view of Azurite Peak and Cascade Crest Trail at Grasshopper Pass

75   WINDY PASS

Easy walk along one of the most spectacular sections of the Cascade Crest Trail, following the boundary line of the North Cascades Primitive Area. Miles of open meadows with scattered groups of larches and other alpine trees, views every step of the way. Ghost town of Barron and sporadically active New Lite Mines in the valley to the west.

Drive through Winthrop up the Methow Valley on Highway 20 for 14 miles; turn right on County Road #23, pass Mazama (Post Office) at ½ mile. Pavement ends in 2½ miles; continue on gravel road 17 miles to Harts Pass. Turn right at the summit onto Slate Peak Road and drive to parking space at first switchback, where the trail begins, or as far as first road-blocking snow patch.

The road being snow-covered doesn't necessarily indicate that the trail is impassable; snow stays later at the trail beginning than almost anyplace else north to Windy Pass. From the road switchback, plod through the snow over a flat promontory from the trail sign, gaining a few feet of altitude, then contour to find snow-free trail.

The route traverses the steep slopes of Slate Peak, within some 300 vertical feet of the summit lookout tower, to enter little Benson Basin, a good campsite. The trail then swings out around a spur ridge, curves back into Buffalo Pass, rounds a corner and crosses a long hillside to 6262-foot

Windy Pass. A superb camp lies near a little pond in the exact top of the pass, amid meadows and larch trees.

For side trips north, take a 1- or 2-hour meadow stroll to the summit of 7307-foot Tamarack Peak or walk the Cascade Crest Trail ½ mile into Windy Basin. Fine views of the Pasayten Range.

The views actually begin on the drive to Harts Pass, with grand vistas down the broad U-shaped glacial trench of the Methow. From the trail the horizon is dominated to east and south by North Gardner Mountain, The Needles, Silver Star, Golden Horn, Tower Mountain, and especially the great mass of Ballard Mountain and Azurite Peak. To west one sees Baker part of the way, but mostly 9070-foot Jack Mountain. Many other valleys, many other peaks.

Before or after going to Windy Pass, one may wish to hike along the road to the summit of Slate Peak and climb the ladders of the lookout tower.

Round trip 7 miles
Allow 5 hours
High point 7200 feet
Elevation gain to Windy Pass 400 feet,
on return 1000 feet
Best late June through October
One day or backpack

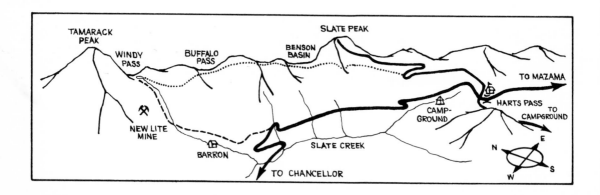

North from Slate Peak towards Windy Pass

76   PARK BUTTE

An overlook of the southwest glaciers of Mount Baker, of the Black Buttes (remnants of a more ancient volcano), of the Twin Sisters, and many other peaks and valleys. Fascinating days can be spent exploring moraines, ancient lake bottoms, glaciers, ridges, rocks, ponds and ice water.

Drive on State Highway 20 to several blocks west of center of Concrete; turn left on Baker Lake road. Go 10 miles to Rocky Creek Bridge; turn left on road to Schrieber's Meadows; go 9 miles to end. (Last ½ mile into logged-off area is muddy, rough, and opens late.) Park in any of several short spur roads left. A trail sign shows way to footlog crossing Sulphur Creek.

The horse-mucked trail ascends gently through the heather-and-flower parkland of sub-alpine Schrieber's Meadows, past a trail shelter, and enters woods. At 1 mile several melt-water streams from Easton Glacier must be boulder-hopped, waded, or crossed on footlogs. Rocky Creek and Sulphur Creek are close together here, and meltwater floods flow into sometimes one, sometimes the other. Look for native sulphur, yellow crystals in whitish rock.

Switchbacks climb steeply through the timber into First Morovitz Meadow. The trail assumes an easier grade en route to Second Morovitz Meadow. Several good campsites near the trail junction here: right fork to Baker Pass, left to Park Butte Lookout, visible to the southwest, and reached by a mile of ridge-walking.

For an exciting side trip, roam east from the trail junction to the summit of Railroad Grade, an old lateral moraine of the Easton Glacier. Look down onto the raw, naked gravel and boulders of the wasteland below the glacier. Follow Railroad Grade easily to an elevation of 6000 feet or more, wander amid ponds, waterfalls, rock buttresses, and meadows, and on to the brink of cliffs falling to the Deming Glacier, a most healthy ice stream.

Round trip 7 miles
Allow 6 hours
High point 5450 feet
Elevation gain 2250 feet
Best July 15 through October
One day or backpack

Late October snowfall covers Park Butte Trail. Mount Baker in distance

Easy hike to the fire lookout atop Sauk Mountain; a remarkable view of the entire Skagit Basin and Mt. Baker region. A nice Sunday walk for families.

Drive on Highway 20 east from Concrete 9 miles to a point just west of Rockport State Park. Turn left (north) at a sign marking Forest Service road #3602 and Sauk Mountain Lookout. Drive 7 steep miles to a road junction immediately below the summit. The main logging road goes ahead to a saddle and down into a valley currently being skinned. The sharp right turn onto a rough "road" may be signed "Lookout", or it may not. Probably necessary to park near the junction and walk the 1/4 mile to sign that announces the trail.

The well-maintained trail climbs in 29 switchbacks up the southwest side of Sauk Mountain to the ridge top, then follows the crest north 3/8 mile through acres of alpine meadows to the lookout. One of the finest views in the entire range—over the valley of the Skagit, out to the lowlands, and into the North Cascades. At night, lights of scattered homes 4000 feet below, and the frightening sky-glow of Pugetopolis south. The only places at all difficult are the several crossings of steep gullies.

A side trail to Sauk Lake leaves the lookout trail soon after the crest is reached. The junction —on the right at the point where the lookout trail turns north—is difficult to see, especially when the greenery is deep. The hiker can find it most easily when returning from the lookout or by glancing back frequently on the way up. Sauk Lake lies in a cirque 1200 feet below. The trail goes southeast for 1/2 mile, then traverses north to a side ridge, where it ducks through a little notch, then makes long arcs down the curve of the basin. The wooded area on the east shore of the little round lake provides the best camps.

Round trip to lookout 3 miles
Allow 2 1/2 hours
High point 5537 feet
Elevation gain 1137 feet
Best July to October
One day or backpack

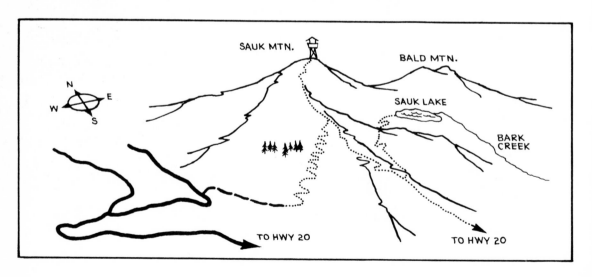

Sauk River from Sauk Mountain Trail. Mount Whitechuck (left) and Mount Whitehorse (extreme right)

Views to all points of the compass: directly down into the Cascade River, off to the nearby Skagit Valley, a full circle over the whole North Cascades, and mountains too numerous to name. Monogram Lake adds a fine side trip or alternative destination.

Drive on State Highway 20 to Marblemount; take Cascade River Road east 7 miles to well-marked parking area and trail.

A 20 per cent grade for the first 2 miles makes this a trail to remember. The hiker seems to be walking in a giant snake track as he slowly climbs the toe of the steep ridge between Lookout and Monogram Creeks. Back and forth the short switchbacks go, mounting a thousand feet with every mile. No water for 3 miles.

At 3½ miles a sign at a trail junction shows Monogram Lake to be 2 miles to the right, the summit of Lookout Mountain 1½ miles to the left.

Gradually the trail works its way up out of the timber; the last mile to the lookout is through meadows. The trail, once more steep, is narrower, too, for the outer edges of the tread have crumbled. Troubles are forgotten, however, when the summit view is reached.

Good campsites in forest at the 3-mile stream; better ones at 4900-foot, meadow-surrounded Monogram Lake at the southern end of Teebone Ridge. An easy stroll to the horseshoe-shaped rim 500 feet above the lake is rewarded with a dramatic look straight at all 8800 feet of Eldorado Peak, 6 miles away.

Round trip to lookout 10 miles
Allow 9 hours
High point 5719 feet
Elevation gain 4519 feet
Best mid-July through October
One day or backpack

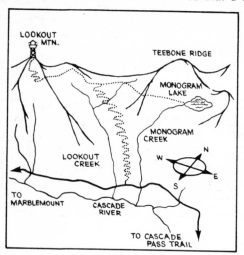

Eldorado Peak from Lookout Mountain

79   HIDDEN LAKE PEAKS

An alpine outrigger extending deep into an angle of the Cascade River valley, providing classic views of the **achtausenders** from Eldorado Peak on the north through Cascade Pass and south along the Ptarmigan Traverse to Dome Peak. Forests below, waterfalls and flowers all around.

Drive on State Highway 20 to Marblemount; take Cascade River Road east to about 2 miles beyond Marble Creek Campground; turn left on Sibley Creek Road and, avoiding logging spurs, go to the end of the driveable road in a big logging patch where there is an obvious place to park. Hike 1/4 mile up the bulldozed track beyond the parking area; trail start is plainly marked.

Switchbacks climb through forest for a bit more than 1 mile. Trail then emerges into an aisle cut through shoulder-high brush thickets and crosses Sibley Creek. (Some years avalanche snow may cover the valley floor at this point. If so, look for obvious trail-cut in the greenery above the snow on the other side of the valley.) More switchbacks in the grass to around 2½ miles, then the trail recrosses the creek and begins a long traverse around the Hidden Lake Peaks. Just at this point note the abrupt contact between metamorphic and granitic rocks, the one supporting grassy-type flora, the other dominated by heather. After about a mile of traverse, the route rounds a corner of the ridge and gains elevation. If snowpatches cover the way, just forge ahead in the direction

the trail has been going—it will be there. At 3½ miles is a miniature basin just below the lookout. (The cabin is visible atop the cliffs.) Here the trail almost vanishes in snow. Follow your nose to the pass overlooking Hidden Lake and broad views of peaks and glaciers.

To this point the hike is easy. The new hiker would be wise to halt here, because the remaining short distance to the summit may **not** be easy or safe: the trail twists in and out between huge granite blocks, and may cross dangerously steep snow on the ridge-crest.

For a dandy side trip, drop down from the pass on snow and talus to Hidden Lake in its meadow-trimmed cirque. For another side trip, or for a shorter hike (about half the distance and time) and one open earlier in the summer, leave the trail where it crosses Sibley Creek the second time and climb straight up the slippery heather meadows a scant ½ mile to Sibley Creek Pass; the view equals or surpasses that from the lookout. Superb campsites all along the upper trail; the miniature basin below the lookout is the best.

Round trip to lookout 8 miles
Allow 6 to 8 hours
High point 6850 feet
Elevation gain 2850 feet
Best late July through October
One day or backpack

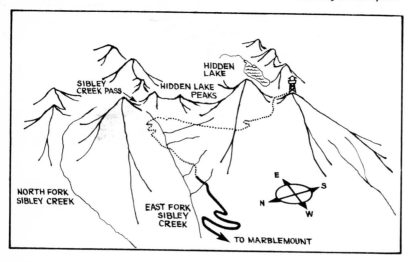

Icebound Hidden Lake and (left to right) Forbidden Peak, Boston Peak, Sahale Peak, Cascade Pass, and Mount Johannesburg

80 CASCADE PASS AND SAHALE ARM

Only 3 hours to the top of the divide at Cascade Pass, where superlative views of the "American Alps" and associated wilderness valleys compete for attention with the nearer perfections of snowy beargrass, brilliant blue lupine, and fiery Indian paintbrush. From the flowered meadows of Sahale Arm, higher up, inspect the long line of summits extending south to Glacier Peak.

Drive on State Highway 20 to Marblemount, cross bridge over the Skagit River and go straight ahead 25 miles on Cascade River road to its scenic terminus. A new trail takes off uphill from parking area.

Cascade Pass has a long history as a cross-mountain route for prospectors, miners, and explorers. The Diamond Claim, located in 1891, is on a side road uphill to the left. The trail to the pass formerly began from this silver-and-lead mine. The new trail leaves the parking area, enters dim forest and close undergrowth, switchbacks uphill, and gradually climbs onto an open hillside of rock buttresses, low plants, and tumbling freshets. The Cascade valley opens out below. Above is the mile-high wall of Johannesberg, with its hanging (and avalanching) glaciers.

At 3.4 miles is Cascade Pass, 5392 feet. The wind blows free here; drop down the east side a little way to the shelter of tree clumps, to rest and admire the valley of the wild Stehekin River, with McGregor Peak and other summits of the Lake Chelan area outlined against the hazy distance.

Turning north from the pass, follow a steep way trail up about ½ mile to a viewpoint down into the big round pool of Doubtful Lake, then continue along the broad, curving ridge which mounts steadily north toward Sahale Peak, 8715 feet. Sooner or later the trail disappears into snowfields and the casual hiker stops; the summit of Sahale is strictly for trained climbers.

It is not unknown for more than 100 people to be encamped overnight at Cascade Pass, a remarkable feat since campsites are few, firewood virtually non-existent, and water, when available, is not plentiful, sanitary, nor convenient. Less-populated campsites can be found at Doubtful Lake or, better still, by a stream-crossing in the shelter or evergreens an easy ½ mile below the summit to the east.

Round trip to Sahale Arm 9-10 miles
Allow 6-8 hours
High point 6000-7000 feet
Elevation gain 2500-3500 feet
Best mid-July through September
One day or backpack

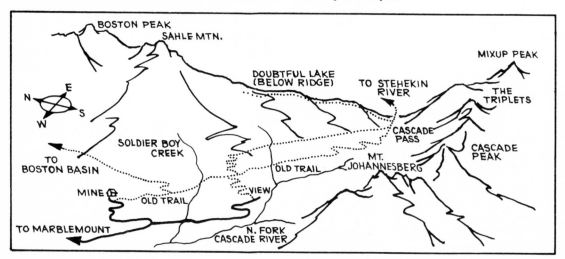

Western Washington fog flowing over Cascade Pass below Mixup Peak

81   STEHEKIN TO CASCADE PASS

An 80-year-old route of explorers, prospectors, and trappers—crossing the Cascade Mountains from arid Columbia hills to Puget Sound lowlands, passing through wilderness little damaged by civilization. The distinctive charm of the Stehekin is largely due to the fact it cannot be reached by automobile (the few there have been barged in).

If traveling from west to east, approach as for Cascade Pass (described elsewhere) and leave the hills via Stehekin Road, a voyage down Lake Chelan, and bus from Chelan. (To minimize road-walking, arrange beforehand to be met at road-end or other way-point by taxi from Stehekin.)

If hiking from east to west, approach as for Park Creek Pass (described elsewhere) and leave the wilds at the end of the Cascade River Road by prearranged car, either parked there before the trip or driven up by a friend to meet the party. Sometimes one can hitch a ride to public transportation by making the acquaintance of fellow hikers at Cascade Pass; Sunday is the best day to try.

To approach from the east, walk 24 miles northwestward from the dock at Stehekin to Cottonwood Camp, at the end of Stehekin Road. Those who wish a shorter walk, or more time for side trips, can hire taxi transportation from Stehekin to the road-end or any intermediate point. Side trips can be made to Agnes Gorge from High Bridge or perhaps—if one has an extra day to spend—north up Rainbow Creek to the Cascade Crest Trail and then down Bridge Creek back to the Stehekin. Good campspots at Company Creek, High Bridge, Bridge Creek, Park Creek, Cottonwood Camp, and Basin Creek.

From Cottonwood Camp the battered remnant of a miners' truck track persists for almost 3 miles to Basin Creek. A long view down the valley from here, and a steep look up into Horseshoe Basin, many waterfalls, and the glaciers of Buckner and Ripsaw Ridge. Beyond Basin Creek the trail traverses an enormous rockslide and then switchbacks up a steep step into the little hanging valley below Cascade Pass.

A small side trail, left (south), .4 mile below the east side of the pass, leads to sheltered camping and plentiful firewood among the trees of Pelton Basin. Camping at the pass is not recommended. From Cascade Pass, make a side trip to Sahale Arm (see description elsewhere) or continue downtrail 3½ miles to the Cascade River Road.

Total distance 29 miles
Allow 3 to 7 days
High point 5392 feet
Elevation gain 2592 feet
Best late July through September
Backpack

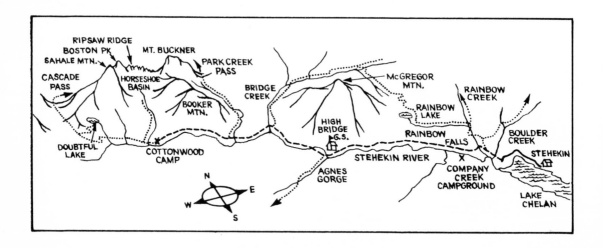

Stehekin River Valley from Sahale Arm

82 SOURDOUGH MOUNTAIN

A fire-lookout view over Ross Dam and Lake to Jack Mountain on the east; south across Diablo Lake to Ruby Mountain, Colonial, Pyramid, and Snowfield Peaks, and Thunder Creek valley all the way to Park Creek Pass; west down Gorge Lake and the Skagit valley and around to the southern edge of the Pickets. On the horizon to the south are Logan, Buckner, and Boston and the huge Boston Glacier.

Drive on State Highway 20 to Diablo Dam. Continue past the powerhouse, park in designated area. Walk three blocks back past the powerhouse to the tennis court. Trail begins in the rockslide behind the court.

In the first 3 miles the trail rises a grueling 3500 feet through heavy forest. Several viewpoints a short distance from the trail—enjoy the scenery while you catch your breath.

At 3 miles the main trail continues straight ahead; the sharp switchback left goes 3/4 mile to Diablo Camp's TV receiving station, a wonderful viewpoint and a suitable turnaround point for a one-day hike. The trail thus far is often free of snow as early as May.

The second 3½ miles gain only 1400 feet along a more open, south-facing slope. Only hikers in good condition should attempt to do the complete trip in one day. Camping places are available lower down the trail but the one at Sourdough Creek, 4½ miles, is best. Water can be found at several other points, but is scarce.

To make a loop trip, go down the trail northeast from the summit to Ross Lake, then south along the shoreline to Diablo, a total of approximately 22 miles.

Round trip 13 miles
Allow 7 hours up
High point 5900 feet
Elevation gain 4900 feet
Best June through October
One day or backpack

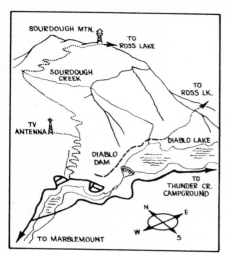

Hikers on Sourdough Mountain overlooking Diablo Lake and Thunder Creek Valley

83   THUNDER CREEK

A trail level for miles, passing through big timber of the type (almost extinct) that made Northwest history, to a valley viewpoint of tall, glaciered peaks. Continues on for many more miles to the source of the creek high amid these same peaks.

Drive State Highway 20 to Diablo Dam, then east approximately 4 miles to Colonial Creek Campground of Mt. Baker National Forest. Trail begins at the upper limit of the campground.

The first few miles of trail are rather flat, through an ancient forest of giant trees. At about 1 mile is a side trail, left, to Fourth of July Pass and Panther Creek. At 5 miles is a shelter, Middle Cabin, just about the point at which a side trail, right, crosses Thunder Creek and starts up McAllister Creek. Near the shelter is an excellent valley view of Logan, Buckner, Boston, Forbidden, and Eldorado, which among them carry half a dozen of the largest glaciers in the North Cascades and countless smaller ones.

Above Middle Cabin the trail is overgrown and not always easy to follow. The trip becomes one for experienced hikers only.

Two miles above the shelter the trail crosses Fisher Creek and shortly thereafter a side trail, left, ascends this creek. The main trail now begins to gain elevation noticeably.

About 10 miles, the two Meadow Cabins provide shelter, with great mountains standing around them in almost a semicircle. The trail begins to climb in earnest, passing close under Mt. Logan during these last miles. At 18 miles is 6040-foot Park Creek Pass, a snow-filled rock-chute amid a stormy sea of mountain whitecaps. Campsites about half a mile below the summit on either side.

The return trip can be made over the same route, or by continuing through Park Creek Pass (see description), returning to civilization west over Cascade Pass (see description) or east by way of Lake Chelan.

Round trip to Middle Cabin 10 miles
Allow 5 hours
High point at Park Creek Pass 6040 feet
Elevation gain to Pass 4800 feet
Best April through November in lowlands, July through September in highlands
One day or backpack

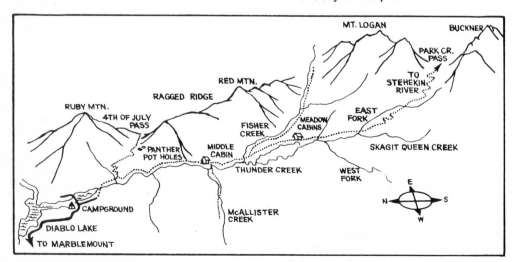

Thunder Creek Trail

Professor Arthur E. Harrison of the University of Washington has been studying the Coleman Glacier since 1950, and in this time it has advanced half a mile down the valley, engulfing small alder trees growing in its path. The advance is measured and recorded by photo-theodolite at 6-month intervals. To provide access to survey stations, Professor Harrison's volunteer crews have blazed several routes which can be used by hardy hikers who don't mind a few inconveniences.

From Bellingham or Deming, drive east on State Highway 542 to approximately 1 mile beyond town of Glacier. Turn right onto Glacier Creek Road and continue some 7 miles to a "Kulshan Cabin Trail" sign, with a large obvious parking area nearby. Walk a short distance to a bridge across Grouse Creek. Beyond it 100 feet is an unmarked path left. The route is well blazed, but can be lost at places if one does not watch carefully. The first mile is through immature forest, curving gradually toward Mt. Baker. Inconveniences include some logs, a few wet places, and Kulshan Creek, which can be crossed by boulder-hopping. The wooded stretch ends at a wonderful viewpoint of the glacier snout about 1 mile away, and the summit of Baker. This is far enough for most people.

The next mile is blazed through a slide area of sparse alder. Then the wild torrent of Heliotrope Creek must be crossed, hopefully on boulders. A thick patch of slide alder follows, and when the hiker breaks out of this thicket he finds himself alongside Glacier Creek. The bank of the stream can be followed to the right to within 1000 feet of the glacier. Stay out of range of rolling rocks and ice; the steep snout is very unstable. A rudimentary bridge has been thrown across the river to enable the scientists to reach their observation points about 1/4 mile on the opposite hillside. The way trail across the bridge also climbs Bastille Ridge for overwhelming views of Baker.

Round trip 4 miles
Allow 3 hours
High point 4700 feet
Elevation gain 1000 feet
Best July through October
One day

Advancing snout of the Coleman Glacier engulfs an alder grove

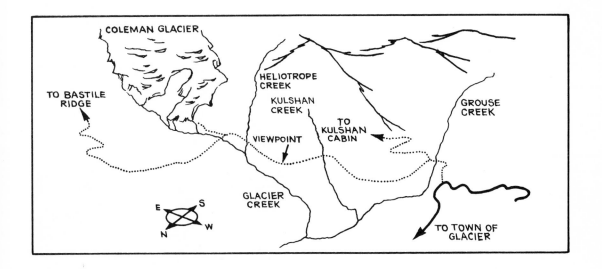

An easy forest walk to a climbers' shelter near timberline, leading to rambles and scrambles on moraines looking up to Mt. Baker and the Black Buttes and down to the chaotic ice of the advancing Coleman Glacier.

Driving directions are as for Coleman Glacier, and the trail beginning is also the same.

The trail traverses and switchbacks 2 miles to Kulshan Cabin, maintained by the Mt. Baker Club and Western Washington Ski Club and open to all whose love of the outdoors brings them this way. Considerate treatment ensures its survival. Above the cabin the trail follows the crest of a moraine a short distance to timberline, then branches into many less-good trails, all leading to snows or meadows, depending on the season. In late summer one may wander in all directions over moraines, creeks, rock buttresses, and flowers. Because of the enormous snowfall on Mt. Baker, earlier than August there may still be snow patches on the trail leading to the cabin, and solid snow above that level.

One of these above-timberline paths leads to Heliotrope Ridge, south about a mile, where at 6000 feet or so the moraine touches ice-polished slabs and permanent snows. Another path, steep and rocky, and confusing in fog or storm, traverses meadows east to a forested moraine where the hiker dodges through very old trees and suddenly finds himself on the brink of a gravel cliff, looking abruptly down to the Coleman Glacier's blue-white chunks of ice.

For those who want time to explore, this is a fine backpack trip. Camping near the cabin is strictly of the slum variety, but there are excellent spots in the meadows above. One, for instance, is on the aforementioned moraine immediately above the Coleman.

Hikers should limit explorations to meadow and rock, no matter how solid the snow or ice appear. On slopes above the cabin, innocent-seeming snow merges with the glacier and covers deep crevasses, some of them only a few feet away from the security of flowered slopes.

Round trip 6 miles
Allow 5 hours
High point 6000 feet
Elevation gain 2300 feet
Best August and September
One day or backpack

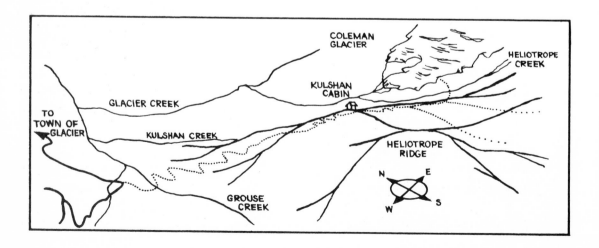

Coleman Glacier from a viewpoint one-half mile beyond Kulshan Cabin

Much reward for little effort. Only 2 trail miles, through meadows all the way, to a 6500-foot summit well-situated for memorable views, particularly of Baker and Shuksan to the south and the Chilliwack Mountains of British Columbia to the north. The Twin Lakes at the base of the peak form a sky-colored carpet.

Drive on State Highway 542 east about 13½ miles beyond Glacier, into Mt. Baker National Forest. A state highway maintenance shed and a small sign mark the Twin Lakes Road, which leaves the left side of the highway, uphill. Climb 7 miles on this steep miners' road, hard on cars and on some drivers' nerves. The road climaxes with five hairpin turns, then enters the lake basin and levels off at 5200 feet. Ample parking space at the end of the narrow causeway of rock and earth separating the lakes; the trail begins at the far end, marked by a rustic sign.

The trail is much used, being short, spectacular, and mostly easy. At ¼ mile is a side trail, right, leading north to Low Pass, High Pass, and Mt. Larrabee. (Superb country, but in many years the trail is blocked year-round by steep snow.) The summit trail switchbacks gradually westward, up lightly forested parkland which becomes increasingly open and dry. At 1¼ miles the path crosses a steep, sandy slope where the footing is very uncertain. If snow covers the trail here, go above or below. Less-confident hikers need help also a short distance beyond, where they may

feel like squeezed lemons as they squirm through a narrow defile. The last half-mile is in the open on loose and sandy rock, well above tree line. A lookout cabin at the summit is manned in fire-season emergencies and commands a wide view.

After descending, one might take a quick dip in upper Twin Lake, although the water is shocking cold even in summer. By camping at Twin Lakes hikers can have time to explore additional trails nearby, and to ramble the inviting green meadows.

Round trip 4 miles
Allow 3 hours
High point 6521 feet
Elevation gain 1321 feet
Best July 15 to October 15
One day

Mount Baker from Winchester Mountain Trail

The ice rarely melts completely from this chilly lakelet. Enclosing meadow ridges offer a classic view of Shuksan, from summit tower to Hell's Highway (Upper Curtis Glacier) to the Lower Curtis Glacier to Shuksan Creek to Baker Lake. On warm days avalanches rumble almost constantly.

Drive on State Highway 542 to Mt. Baker Lodge, then 1 more mile to Austin Pass, or as far as the road is open. (Frequently one cannot drive beyond the Lodge until August.) A sign on the left marks parking space and the trail, which is closed to wheels.

The path drops an abrupt 800 feet into the headwaters of Swift Creek, then follows around the slope, through meander-twined meadows (good camping) overcrowded with marmots and into pleasant woods on a long flat traverse. At 2 miles (benchmark, 3930 feet) is the lowest elevation of the trip. Here a brook babbles through a meadow (another camp).

The trail now begins a 900-foot climb. Heather and scattered trees to start, a granite rockslide infested with conies, and around a forested corner into a little valley, at the head of which lies the saddle to the lake. In early summer the valley may be full of snow, in which case simply forge ahead and up. Later it opens into a glory of waterfalls and chunks of rock and bits of meadow and snow

Even in late summer it may be necessary to scramble over a snow cornice to reach the saddle

with the lake immediately below and Shuksan above. The only problem now is deciding what to do first, and what to do next. A day is not enough; a week is adequate for an introduction.

In early summer, with snow all about, the best camps are atop the low ridge separating the lake from the creek that flows between the lake and Shuksan. Later on the lake outlet and the in-between valley are better.

Perhaps the first walk to take is a circumnavigation of Lake Ann, noting the contacts between granitic rocks and the complex metamorphics of which Shuksan is constructed. In autumn the blueberries may lead one upward on the ridge of Mt. Ann. From the saddle, wander up a spur left to Shuksan Arm, atop which lies a secret camp in a tiny basin.

The best side trip of all dips on the trail into the inbetween valley, then switchbacks to a place where climbers have beaten a track steep left—the summit route. Just here nature has obliterated a few yards of CCC trail built in the 1930s; scramble across steep gravel to pick up the tread and walk easily on to a turnaround promontory a few yards from the ice.

Round trip 7 miles
Allow 6-8 hours
High point 4800 feet
Elevation loss 800 feet, gain 900 feet
Best August to October
One day or backpack

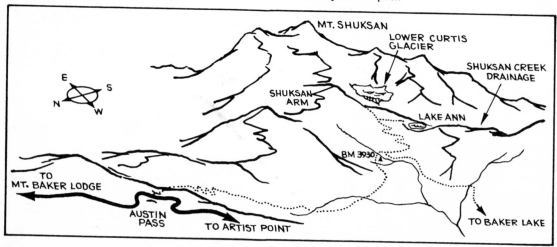

Curtis Glacier and Mount Shuksan from Lake Ann campsite

88 TABLE MOUNTAIN

Hike over Table Mountain, a high plateau of meadow and rock offering a fine view of Baker, Shuksan, and other peaks, then circle around to the starting point without retracing steps. A favorite fall-color trip.

Drive on State Highway 542 east 2 miles beyond Mt. Baker Lodge, to the parking area at end of the road on Kulshan Ridge. (Or drive as far as snow allows.) Trail is easily located, continuing west from road.

Easy traveling for ¼ mile along the open ridge to a junction with the return trail. Then right, cautiously, on a series of short zig-zags ascending 500 feet up the eastern extension of Table Mountain, whose slopes here are dangerously steep. In less than 30 minutes the hiker is on the summit, a half-mile expanse of open mountain meadow, with snow pools for accent. One in particular of these pools, on the south end of the plateau, remains through September and forms a most attractive natural "reflecting pool." The summit of Mt. Baker is only 6 miles away and Shuksan is equally prominent; many lesser North Cascades peaks are also on display.

The east-to-west route across the flat summit is over a large steep snowfield, frequently difficult and dangerous to cross; if so, hikers unequipped with ice axes should turn back. From the west end of Table Mountain the trail descends to the north, crosses a lower plateau, and zig-zags towards Mt. Baker down the western

projection of the mountain, somewhat as it did at the beginning, but less steeply. At the foot is a trail junction. The trail to the left completes the 3½-mile Table Mountain Loop by contouring back along the base of the mountain to the beginning.

The trail to the right leads 1½ miles into wooded country to the Galena Chain Lakes: four lakes of varying sizes strung along the mountainside almost on a level with one another. The best sites for overnight camping are found here, sheltered by the trees. Along the way the roar of Mazama Falls can be heard and a trail toward it down Wells Creek appears shortly to the left. The falls and its beautiful setting are well worth visiting if one has time and energy to hike this trail a mile or so each way.

On the homeward trip one can return along the above-mentioned route around the base of Table Mountain, or follow a route east through Herman Pass (view of Shuksan), and down past the Bagley Lakes to Mt. Baker Lodge, about 3½ miles.

Round trip 3½ miles
Allow 3 hours
High point 5742 feet
Elevation gain 600 feet
Best in September
One day or backpack

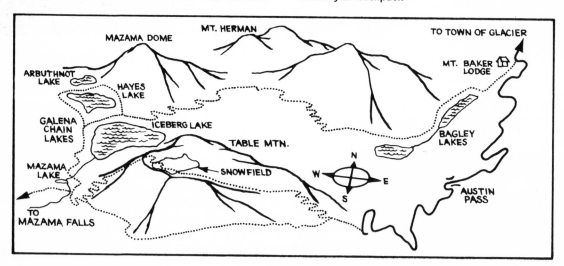

Iceberg Lake and Herman Saddle

Thousands of snow geese winter on tidelands of the Skagit River. Great flocks rise from the salt marshes, shift position, and settle down again. A levee across the tidelands leads out toward open water of Skagit Bay. All around, seemingly without end, stretch irregular brush patches, shrubby trees, and marsh-meadows. From the wide path atop the levee hikers can watch not only vast numbers of the visiting snow geese, but many other types of bird life as well.

Silvery hordes of dunlins, a shore-dwelling bird, appear and disappear in mid-air as they wheel and flash-turn with startling speed. The dainty short-eared owl, a day-hunting species, floats close to the ground like a miniature glider on buff-marked silent wings, circling cattail- and sedge-lined pockets and soaring swiftly over the low dikes which delineate them. The bald eagle hovers high above or perches at a vantage point, distinguished by his white head and rump. Snowy owls, infrequent visitors from the Arctic, choose locations slightly raised above their surroundings and remain there patiently, turning their heads occasionally in slow, almost complete circles as they seek the birds and small animals which form

their food. Marsh wrens, great blue herons, red-wing blackbirds, marsh hawks, bufflehead ducks, killdeer, savannah sparrows, and song sparrows are among many other species the alert visitor can identify.

Drive to Conway, a few miles south of Mt. Vernon, and go west through Conway and across the South Fork of the Skagit River to Fir Island. Approximately 1½ miles from Conway is a sign, "Public Hunting," indicating a turn left (south). Drive about a mile to the end of the road and the entrance of the 12,500-acre Skagit Game Range. Hikers would best stay away during the shooting season, October 15-January 15.

Just past Range Manager's headquarters the road crosses Wiley Slough to a "T" intersection. The walkers' road, closed by a locked chain, goes right; parking is to the left. After leaving the car, walk back along the roadway, then continue on the closed road along the dike beside Wiley Slough. The open water of Skagit Bay is just discernible ahead. On either side stretch the tidal flats, merging gradually to landward with level, cultivated fields.

After walking perhaps ¾ mile, at a junction with another dike, a small pond is reached, below

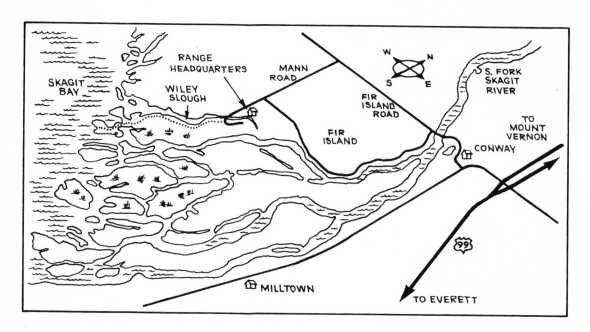

Wiley Slough

the dike right. There is the possibility of photographing Mt. Baker reflected in its waters. Fine views from dike junction: to the west Olympic peaks beyond Camano and Whidbey Islands; farther north, Mt. Erie, and next to it a column of smoke rising from industrial Anacortes; to the northeast, Mt. Baker, and many other Cascade peaks south to Three Fingers and Pilchuck. The dike continues and becomes a true footpath. One may stroll to the end, near the bay shore, exploring at will along the way.

Round trip 2 miles
Allow 2 hours
High point 15 feet
Elevation gain 0 feet
Best February through September
One day

90 AYRES POINT TO DEWATTO

A moderately rough beach hike along Hood Canal with fine views of the Olympic Mountains and a long reach of salt water as well. Accessible year round. One of the most uninhabited Puget Sound beaches reachable by car; as of 1966, only a few summer cottages along the 6 miles.

Drive from Bremerton or Shelton on State Highway 3 to Belfair; take State Highway 300 past Belfair State Park and continue on county road through Tahuya to a mile beyond Ayres Point, where paving ends. Park at roadside. A gravel road extends north from Tahuya to Dewatto, at the north end of the beach. If two cars are available, one can be parked at Dewatto before starting the hike.

Plan the hike schedule after consulting a tide table for Hood Canal; the beach is passable only at moderately low tides and is completely blocked at high tides. Landmarks along the way are Musqueti Point at ½ mile, Cougar Spit at 1½ miles, and Red Bluff at 3 miles. Make Red Bluff the turnaround point, or continue north another 3 miles to Dewatto. About 4 miles are the remains of an old log chute from Aldrich Lake, used by early loggers to slide timber from the lake into the channel. Across the water is the Lake Cushman area of Olympic National Forest, and the green and white heights of Mt. Washington and Mt. Ellinor (described elsewhere).

Most Puget Sound beaches are privately owned. However, it is customary to allow the public to walk on any saltwater beach—a walking privilege only, it should be noted. Clam-digging, picnicking, and camping are solely by permission of the property owners. If access is specifically denied, as through signs posted on the beach, the rights of the owners to restrict the use of their property should be respected.

For a good picnic spot, drive to Aldrich Lake (near Robbins Lake) about 2 miles south of Dewatto. On state lands here a beautiful picnic area is provided, overlooking Hood Canal on one side and the lake on the other. No drinking water, however, either at the lake or on the beach.

Round trip 10 miles or less
Allow 5 hours
High point 10 feet
Elevation gain 10 feet
All seasons good
One day

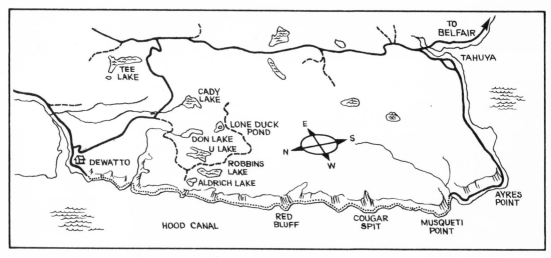

Cloud-shrouded Mount Ellinor and Mount Washington from Dewatto on Hood Canal

91   MT. ELLINOR

Named in 1856 for Ellinor Fauntleroy of Seattle, this peak has probably the most accessible summit in the Olympics. A panorama from the summit, of Hood Canal and Puget Sound waterways, of the Cascades from Mt. Rainier north to Whitehorse and Three Fingers, and of Olympic National Park. The original surveyors of the Olympics, Arthur Dodwell and Theodore F. Rixon, climbed this peak for a preliminary orientation before entering the unmapped interior.

Drive on US 101 to Hoodsport; turn west on Lake Cushman Road for 8 miles. At junction, turn right for 1½ miles, then left on Big Creek Road 5 miles. Sign indicates start of trail; ample parking nearby.

Logging activity in the Big Creek Basin of Olympic National Forest has shortened the trail considerably from what it once was. However, 2½ miles still remain, mostly through forest, very rough but passable. The grade is easy at first; the final two-thirds is steep. Watch for a viewpoint about halfway up where one can look out through the timber down onto Lake Cushman. The trail ends at timberline—and a superlative view of Puget Sound.

On the high, open slopes the route is easy for an experienced hiker to follow, but beginners could get lost. Above meadows, scramble up a large, open gully, staying out of the fall-line of rocks dislodged by people ahead. Turn left at the top, go over one lower ridge; it is then but a short distance to the summit. Remember that the frequent fog, in which it is easy to lose the way, is a hazard to be respected.

The most remarkable feature of the view eastward is Mt. Rainier, directly across the Nisqually Reach, often seen above smog obscuring the lowlands. On clear days both Tacoma and Seattle are visible, with their long backdrop of Cascade Mountains from Mt. St. Helens to Glacier Peak. The Puget Sound country can be seen as well from timberline trail-end as from the mountain top, but views into the interior of the Olympic Peninsula are reserved for those who reach the summit. Beyond neighboring Mt. Washington, whose profile resembles that of our first President, are jumbled 1400 square miles of peaks and valleys. Among them, not prominent and almost 30 miles away, Mt. Olympus can be distinguished by the exceptional mass of snow it carries.

Round trip 6 miles
Allow 4 hours
High point 5944 feet
Elevation gain 3000 feet
Best July through September
One day

Mount Rainier rising above the Puget Sound country from Mount Ellinor

A forest trail to a pair of alpine lakes close under the Sawtooths, a line of peaks composed largely of "pillow lava"—molten rock extruded into the waters of an ancient sea and now uplifted and eroded into strange shapes with outcrops of interesting minerals. For broader views of this southeast corner of Olympic National Park, follow the trail to the meadows of Gladys Pass.

Drive on US 101 north from Olympia to Hoodsport, then left to Lake Cushman and up the North Fork of the Skokomish River. Park near the end of the road, about 3 miles beyond Staircase Ranger Station. Trail sign on the right.

The way to the lakes is entirely through forest (nice and cool in hot weather). Not particularly steep, but a steady and unwavering climb. At 3½ miles is a fork left (north) to Black-and-White Lakes and Smith Lake. The fork to Flapjack Lakes goes right, and in another ½ mile or so reaches the lakes, one quite shallow and marshy, the other deeper and boulder-studded, the two separated only by a narrow isthmus. Good camping at many places around the shores, the most scenic being on the isthmus. Climbers often basecamp here for Sawtooth ascents. A rehabilitated shelter built some 25 years ago gives cover in case of need.

For more meadows and wider views, continue up the trail another 1½ miles and 1000 vertical feet to Gladys Pass, between Mt. Gladys and Cruiser Peak. Lush wildflowers in season and frequent tarns; if time allows, wander upward through the grass to the summit of Gladys. Cruiser Peak, 6104 feet, stands like a giant boundary monument on the line between Olympic National Forest and Olympic National Park. Its distinctive tower is visible from Seattle.

Round trip to lakes 8½ miles
Allow 8 hours
High point 4000 feet at lakes
Elevation gain 2500 feet
Best July 15 to October 15
One day or backpack

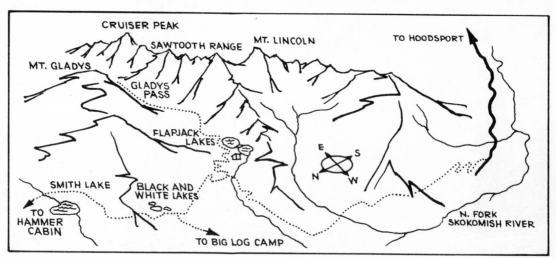

Mount Lincoln and Upper Flapjack Lake

93 UPPER LENA LAKE

Lower Lena Lake, tucked among the trees of Olympic National Forest, is easily reached on an excellent trail along a lovely creek through splendid forests. Upper Lena Lake, 4 miles away, lies in the less-frequented and much quieter alpine country of Olympic National Park. Good camping and fishing at both.

Drive north on US 101 from Olympia to Eldon. Turn left on Hamma Hamma River Road. Park about ½ mile beyond Phantom Creek; trail sign on the right.

The old trail was plenty good enough, but the Forest Service has constructed a new one of unnecessarily gentle grade and unnecessary length. It is now 2 miles to Lower Lena Lake and another ½ mile to a shelter on the northwest shore. The lake is fed by two forks of Lena Creek, the east flowing from The Brothers, one of the most prominent features of the Olympic horizon from Seattle, and the west, from Mt. Bretherton, entering the lake close by the shelter.

Near the shelter the trail divides, one fork (mainly used by fishermen and climbers) going east and north to The Brothers, the other northerly to Upper Lena Lake. To here the ascent is gradual; beyond, the going to the upper lake gets steep and rough and can only be negotiated on foot.

Just past 3½ miles the trail leaves Olympic National Forest and enters Olympic National Park. Scooters, dogs, and guns must stop here.

Continuing upward, the trail's destination seems to be either Mt. Lena or Mt. Bretherton, both close to 6000 feet, but the actual goal is a pocket between the two peaks. Gradually the trees get shorter, the heather and huckleberries lush; then suddenly the steep trail goes flat, entering the cirque of 4600-foot Upper Lena Lake, fenced in closely, north and south, by the summits of Lena and Bretherton.

The trail to Lower Lena Lake is passable any time of year except dead of winter or very early spring, when it may be snow-covered. Snow remains on the trail to Upper Lena Lake until early summer.

Round trip 12 miles
Allow 8 hours
High point 4600 feet
Elevation gain 3900 feet
Best July through October
One day or backpack

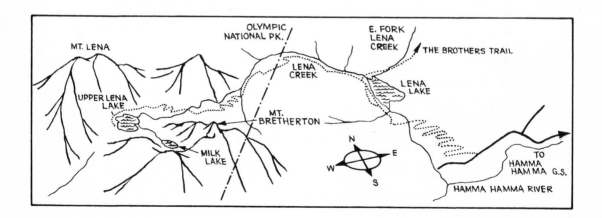

Upper Lena Lake and Mount Bretherton

A long, strenuous trip to an emergency fire lookout with sweeping views; similar views along most of the trail. Hike in late May and early June to see rhododendrons in bloom at the lower levels. Huckleberries, both red and blue, ripen in late summer.

Drive beside Hood Canal on US 101 to .8 mile north of the Duckabush River (about 200 feet south of a sign, "Black Point Road"); turn west on Mt. Jupiter road #262 (no sign), go 3.6 miles; take left fork at sign "Mt. Jupiter Trail— 3", proceed 2.9 miles westerly, park at switchback where a sign marks Mt. Jupiter trail. Two passes may be required to negotiate some turns on the fairly steep road.

Crossing state property the first mile, the trail climbs by a series of switchbacks on the south side of the ridge between the Duckabush and Dosewallips Rivers. Olympic National Forest is entered as the trail reaches the ridge crest, which is then followed west to the summit lookout. The ridge crest rises and falls, so the trail dips up and down too, and the last mile is very steep. Carry water: early in the season there may be dribbles from melting snowbanks, but then steep snowfields make the high levels too difficult for the casual hiker; after July 1 the snow has gone, except for pockets which persist near the lookout and supply water until early August.

Wait for clear weather; the views are the attraction. Northward the scene is the Dosewal-lips valley and the peaks beyond, including Constance; south, across the Duckabush valley, The Brothers and other peaks; east, across Hood Canal, Seattle and the Puget Sound country.

Round trip 14 miles
Allow 10 hours
High point 5701 feet
Elevation gain 3600 feet
Best July through October
One day

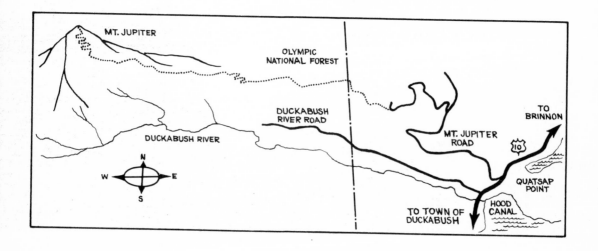

The Brothers and fog-filled Duckabush Valley from Mount Jupiter Trail

95 LAKE CONSTANCE

A magnificent tarn set in alpine trees and meadows, nestled under the cliffs of an arm of Mt. Constance. Famous for mountain goats, whose wool clings everywhere to the heather and trees. The hiker needs goat-like characteristics on a trail legendary among climbers as being more difficult than the ascent of Constance itself, for which the lake is the customary basecamp.

Drive on US 101 along Hood Canal; turn west on the Dosewallips River Road north of Brinnon. Go 14 miles to Constance Creek, just within Olympic National Park. The trail, signed, takes off to the right just west of the creek; parking area a few hundred feet beyond.

The first mile gains some 2000 feet; no switchbacks worth mentioning, just steady and straight up. The second mile gains less altitude but seems even steeper. At several places one must use hands to climb short rock cliffs, and at others must clamber up ladderways of roots polished smooth by generations of travelers. These pitches certainly cannot be called "walking" but fortunately are short. The steepness is not a hazard on the way up, but demands great caution on the descent.

From the lake a climbers' trail leads north up the talus into Avalanche Canyon, a mile-long glacier trough between the east and west peaks of Constance. Geologically, the entire area is a contact zone between sediments and basalt. The canyon is a solemn, impressive place of sharp crags and long screes, with immense walls of "pillow lava" (formed by molten lava emerging under the sea, then cooling abruptly into rounded shapes). Many weird rocks, including fault breccias composed of metamorphosed limestone chunks in gay pastel colors. Green epidote appears as fine crystals, sometimes mixed with sparkling white quartz or calcite. (Remember that rock collecting is not permitted within a National Park.)

Campers can almost count on seeing goats, which visit the lake at night to search for salty edibles, or even in daylight when the resident humans are few and quiet. Watch the cliffs above or visit Avalanche Canyon to see the entire band, complete with frisky kids, walk nonchalantly over precipices that would bother the bravest climber.

A grand backpack, though hauling loads up the steep pitches is hard work. A short level stretch at the 1-mile marker provides a good forest campsite. The best camps are at the lake.

The trip is **not** suitable for beginning hikers, children, or older people, and is distinctly dangerous in places.

Round trip to lake 4 miles
Allow 6 hours
High point 4750 feet at lake
Elevation gain 3300 feet to lake
Best August and September
One day or backpack

Lake Constance

The middle of a string of glacier-basin lakes in the high alpine country of Grand Valley. Particularly good as a beginner backpack trip, since the valley offers fine campsites and the trail obligingly goes downhill on the way in, when packs are usually heaviest.

Drive south from Port Angeles to Hurricane Ridge in Olympic National Park. Just before reaching the lodge turn left onto a narrow un-improved road which follows the crest of Hurricane Ridge for 8½ miles.

The trail begins at end of road and follows the meadowy crest of Lillian Ridge south for the first mile, then turns east and drops steeply for 1400 feet, still on open shale slopes, into Grand Valley. In the light forest of the valley floor, at 3½ miles, is a junction with the Badger Valley and Grand Lake Trail, left, leading in .3 mile to the shelter at Grand Lake.

To Moose Lake, the trail continues right (south) for another ½ mile. Tiny Gladys Lake is .6 mile farther on. Wildflowers hereabouts are at their best in July. Fine roaming through park-land, among waterfalls and snowfields, to the valley head, and easy scrambling to the summit of a 6701-foot peak.

To return, one can make a loop trip by going back to Grand Lake and traveling north down-stream 2 miles, then west up Badger Valley to-ward Obstruction Point. Watch for marmots while ascending Badger Valley. Almost at Obstruction Point, at the head of the valley, the trail meets the one from Deer Park and continues to the road-end starting point.

Total distance 8½ miles
Allow 6 hours
High point 6450 feet
Elevation gain to lake 300 feet, loss 1450 feet
Elevation loss on return 1000 feet, gain 2150 feet
Best July through October
One day or backpack

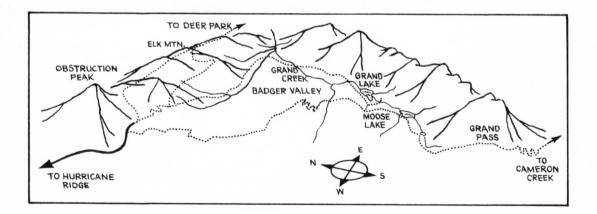

Moose Lake and Grand Valley

97   HIGH DIVIDE

Up through Soleduck forests to meadow country dotted with lakes, then onward and upward to the High Divide and views down to rain forests of the Hoh, across to glaciers of Olympus, and out to the Pacific Ocean.

Drive on US 101 to about 2 miles west of Fairholm at the west end of Lake Crescent; turn left onto Soleduck Road and continue into Olympic National Park. Park at road end, where the trail begins.

The first mile is along the Soleduck River to Soleduck Falls, where the river plunges into a slot-gorge, misty and mossy. A nearby shelter stands at the junction with the Deer Lake trail. From this junction one can make a long one-day or easy overnight trip up past Deer Lake to Bogachiel Ridge, or hike the complete High Divide loop in either direction. The clockwise loop is recommended and described here.

Going clockwise on the loop, the next several miles up the Soleduck River Trail pass through a deep-green virgin forest of hemlock and fir. At 5 miles Appleton Pass trail branches left and the Soleduck Trail crosses the river and climbs steeply to the meadows and silver forest of Soleduck Park and Heart Lake.

At 8½ miles is the crest of the High Divide. To the left the trail runs the ridge east 4 miles to a dead-end on the south side of Cat Peak, first through mountain hemlock and subalpine fir, then breaking out for clear views of the Bailey and Olympus Ranges.

Right and west from the Soleduck junction the High Divide Trail touches a succession of viewpoints. Hoh Lake Trail descends left at about 10½ miles; also at this point a spur trail mounts Bogachiel Peak, from whose summit can be seen the ocean far to the west.

The trail continues westerly along the Bogachiel Ridge, around 11½ miles passing the side trail down into Seven Lakes Basin. Lingering snow may make difficulties for beginning hikers on a series of short switchbacks on the west side of Bogachiel Peak. Look down into Bogachiel Basin to see (as often as not) a large herd of elk. From a forested saddle marked by the ruins of Minnie's Cabin, the trail descends northward into trees, opening briefly on meadows near Deer Lake. At 18½ miles is Soleduck Falls once more, and in another mile the road. A swim in Soleduck Hot Springs is now worth consideration.

Along the way are possibilities beyond mention for overnight camps near the river, atop the High Divide, and beside the many lakes.

Total loop distance 20 miles
Allow 3 days
High point 5474 feet
Elevation gain 4000 feet
Best August through October
Backpack

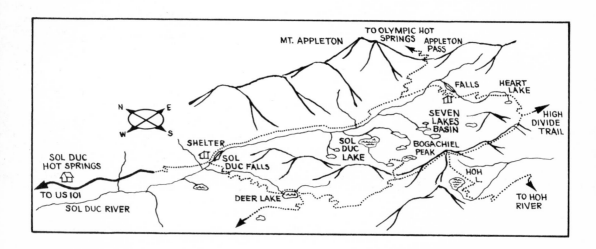

Bluebells on the High Divide. Mount Olympus and Mount Tom in the distance

A short and easy walk on an almost level trail into the heart of the Olympic National Park rain forest, where western hemlock, Sitka spruce, Douglas fir, and western red cedar grow to great size in optimum conditions.

Drive on US 101 south from Forks, go left on Hoh River road to the road-end parking lot. Trail starts as part of the nature trail near the information center.

Heavy foot traffic in the vicinity of the Hoh Ranger Station and Campground has made it necessary to blacktop the paths, but one need not go far from the sound of automobiles to experience the true rain forest spirit. Giant trees grow up to 300 feet tall, with an understory of smaller trees, shrubs, ferns, and mosses. Newcomers are usually surprised to find that despite vigorous plant life the forest is lighter and more open than they expected.

The trail is like a soft sidewalk, except where churned to mud by elk or horses, or where blocked by windfalls—which usually are cut through in early summer.

Now and then the Hoh River can be seen from the trail. Mt. Tom, to the right across the river, is glimpsed at about 2 miles; ½ mile farther a trail takes off right, fords the river, and ascends Tom Creek, passing Mt. Tom Shelter. The world's largest known Sitka spruce tree, 51½ feet in circumference, stands beside the Hoh at 3½ miles.

Fast walkers can make Happy Four Shelter in 2 hours, but it is better to take longer and savor the trip. Between the road and the shelter there are no official campsites, but suitable space and surroundings exist beside the river at 1 mile and 2 miles, and at a stream in the forest about ½ mile beyond Happy Four Shelter. The really superior location, however, is between 4½ and 5 miles, where the Hoh River has abandoned one stream bed and is busily cutting away the bank to make a new one. On the resulting meadow-island a grassy park spreads for half a mile under the alders.

The trail continues beyond Happy Four to Glacier Meadows near the foot of the Blue Glacier on Mt. Olympus; this destination, 18 miles from the road, is a long 1-day, better 2-day hike.

Round trip 11 miles
Allow 6 hours
High point 800 feet
Elevation gain 225 feet
All seasons good
One day or backpack

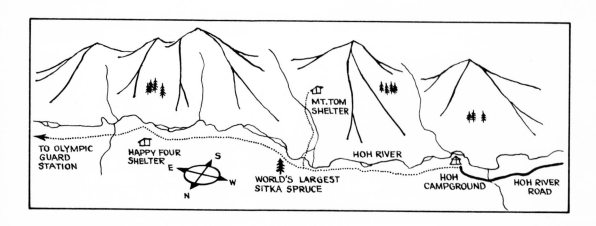

Roosevelt elk grazing in the Hoh River Valley

One of the nation's few remaining primitive beaches, unspoiled, undeveloped, accessible only by foot or boat. Part of the Pacific Coast Area of Olympic National Park.

Drive on US 101 to 2 miles north of Forks; turn west on La Push road 8 miles; turn right on Rialto Beach road 5 miles to parking lot at the beach. No trail, just walk north beside the surf. Be sure to obtain a tide chart beforehand and use it to plan each day's travel.

About half the distance is easy, level, and smooth, as at the beginning. Stout shoes are required, however, for there are also shingles, cobbles (sometimes embellished with barnacles and slippery seaweed), creeks to be waded, headlands to be scrambled over. Creeks and seeps provide fresh though somewhat unattractive "brown water", colored by organic solutes. Camp on the beach or in the ever-adjacent forest.

North of Ellen Creek, Cake Rock is easily recognized among the many offshore seastacks. At 1½ miles is the first headland, which can be either rounded at low tide or climbed over. Cape Johnson, at 3 miles, can be passed only by going around the shore at low tide; a party must adjust its timetable to this requirement. At 5 miles a point must be climbed over, but the trail is not difficult. Immediately beyond the Cedar Creek ford, at 6½ miles, a point can be rounded at low tide or climbed over on a steep and rough trail.

At 7½ miles a trail from the beach leads inland past a reminder of the numerous shipwrecks, the Norwegian Memorial, and then continues to Allen's Bay on Lake Ozette. Yellow Banks, at 13½ miles, is a slide area which must be rounded at low tide, forcing a second adjustment of the hiker's timetable to that of the sea. At 15 miles (shelter) a trail heads inland to Ericson's Bay on Lake Ozette. At Sand Point, ½ mile north, shelters stand near the terminus of still another trail, this leading 3 miles to the resort, ranger station, and campground at the end of Lake Ozette Road.

Indian petroglyphs can be seen at Wedding Rocks, 17 miles. A trail over a narrow strip of land behind the rocks is the only way to pass beyond the point at high tide to hike the final 1½ miles to the end of Olympic National Park north of Cape Alava.

For an excellent one-day hike along a 9-mile triangular route, combine the Sand Point trail, the beach, and an old partly log-paved trail leading inland 3½ miles from the ruins of an Indian village at Cape Alava to Ozette Ranger Station.

One way 22 miles
Allow 3 days
High point 100 feet
Elevation gain 100 feet
All seasons good
Backpack

Wedding Rock near Cape Alava

Hiking near Cape Johnson

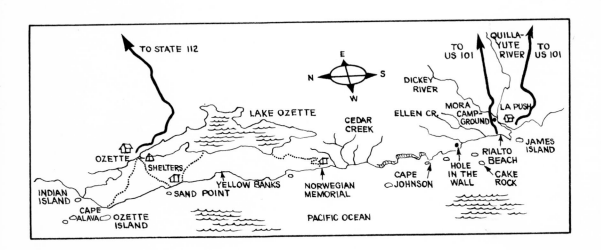

A 50-mile stretch of Pacific Ocean shoreline is preserved in its primitive condition as part of Olympic National Park. The southern section is a shorter but in some ways more challenging hike than the northern. Similar scenery, same closeness of forest and ocean, equally fascinating animal and plant life—but more difficult trails, best-suited to experienced hikers.

Drive on US 101 to 2 miles north of Forks; turn west on LaPush Road 12 miles; sign on left marks spur road to Third Beach Trail. Since considerable vandalism has been experienced at this parking area, it is recommended that cars not be left here overnight; the unfortunate but safer alternative, arranging guarded parking at LaPush, adds a half-hour or so of road-walking to the trip. Hike 1 mile to beach, then south along shore.

In less than a mile leave the beach to cross Taylor's Point. Look for large "X" mark on a white signboard nailed to a tree. Route is marked with red and orange metal tabs. The trail runs partly along logs, partly through windfalls and brush. Trail returns to the beach at 2 miles. (Do not yield to the temptation to hike around Taylor's Point, which can be done only at a minus tide when the surf is modest.) In another ½ mile is a point which must be climbed over at high tide only, regaining the beach at the mouth of Scott Creek. A second point, immediately south, can be rounded on an outgoing tide. At 4½ and 5½ miles are Strawberry and Toleak Points,

neither of which presents a problem.

After crossing Jackson Creek, watch for a trail at 6½ miles leading inland to a crossing of Falls and Goodman Creeks. Cliffs along the shore necessitate this detour. The way is thereafter along the beach, interrupted at 10 miles by a ford, at low tide, of Mosquito Creek. At 10½ miles climb over a point; at 10.9 miles climb another, and at 11.1 miles round another at low tide (climbing is possible but requires great effort). A good sandy beach extends south to Hoh Head, except for two points which can be climbed by marked trail but are preferably passed at low tide. At 12 miles a side trail leads up and over Hoh Head, after which the way continues south along beach. The last point, at 13½ miles, a huge jumble of rocks, can be rounded if the tide is low. From the rocks a narrow strip of beach extends more than 1 mile south to the mouth of the Hoh River, from where side trails lead inland to the end of the Oil City Road, 12 miles from US 101.

For a one-way hike, arrange in advance for transportation. The alternative is to retrace the route.

One way 16 miles
Allow 3 days
High point 200 feet
Elevation gain 200 feet
All seasons good
Backpack

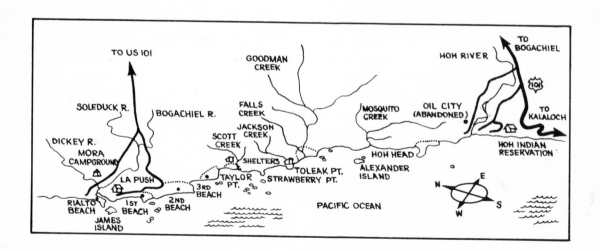

Toleak Point and Graveyard of the Giants

INDEX TO TRIPS AND ALTERNATE DESTINATIONS

LENGTH OF TRIPS
(See text for details)

SHORT HIKES

4. Annette Lake
9. Commonwealth Basin
10. Snoqualmie Lake
12. Mount Margaret
13. Box Canyon
14. Wallace Falls
15. Lake Serene
16. Heybrook Lookout
20. Trout Lake
34. Red Top Mountain
35. High Rock Lookout
35. Bertha May Lakes
37. Lake George

39. Klapatche Park
40. Pinnacle Saddle
41. Paradise Ice Caves
43. Lake Eunice
46. Burroughs Mountain
47. Naches Peak
48. Mount Pete
50. Sourdough Gap
52. Blankenship Meadows
54. Shoe Lake
58. Cedar Creek Camp
59. Mount Pilchuck
63. Poodle Dog Pass
64. Glacier Basin

65. Meadow Mountain
   (first viewpoint)
68. Goat Lake
71. Buck Creek Pass
   (first meadow)
77. Sauk Mountain
80. Cascade Pass
83. Thunder Creek
86. Winchester Mountain
88. Table Mountain
89. Wiley Slough
90. Ayres Point to Dewatto
93. Lower Lena Lake

DAY HIKES

1. Tiger Mountain
2. Mount Si
3. McClellan Butte
5. Granite Mountain
6. Pratt Lake
7. Melakwa Lake
8. Snow Lake
10. Snoqualmie Basin
12. Lake Lillian
17. Lake Blanca
18. Barclay Lake
19. Evergreen Mountain
21. Surprise Lake
22. Lake Josephine
23. Lake Valhalla
24. Alpine Lookout
29. Davis Peak
30. Paddy-Go-Easy Pass
31. Squaw Lake

32. Hyas Lake
33. Long's Pass
36. Indian Henrys
37. Gobblers Knob
38. Emerald Ridge
42. Moraine Park
43. Tolmie Peak
44. Spray Park
45. Summerland
46. Burroughs Mountain
47. Dewey Lake
49. Norse Peak
51. Nelson Ridge
52. Tumac Mountain
53. Cougar Lakes
55. Packwood Lake
58. St. Helens Lake
60. Mount Forgotten
61. Mount Dickerman
62. Gothic Basin

66. Kennedy Hot Springs
74. Azurite View
75. Windy Pass
76. Park Butte
78. Lookout Mountain
79. Hidden Lake Peak
80. Sahale Arm
82. Antenna Station
83. Middle Cabin
84. Coleman Glacier
85. Kulshan Cabin
87. Lake Ann
88. Table Mountain Loop
91. Mount Ellinor
92. Flapjack Lakes
94. Mount Jupiter
95. Lake Constance
96. Moose Lake
98. Happy Four Shelter

STRENUOUS DAY HIKES

10. Lake Dorothy
13. Rampart Ridge
18. Eagle Lake
51. Mount Aix
57. Adams Glacier Camp
65. Meadow Mountain
67. Mount Pugh
82. Sourdough Mountain
94. Mount Jupiter Summit

DAY HIKES THAT MAKE GOOD OVERNIGHT TRIPS

4. Annette Lake
6. Pratt Lake
7. Melakwa Lake
8. Snow Lake
10. Lake Dorothy
12. Lake Lillian
13. Rampart Ridge
17. Lake Blanca
18. Barclay Lake
20. Foss Lakes
21. Surprise Lake
22. Lake Josephine
23. Lake Valhalla
35. Bertha May Lakes
36. Indian Henrys
37. Gobblers Knob
39. Klapatche Park
45. Summerland
47. Dewey Lake
49. Lake Basin
52. Tumac Mountain
53. Cougar Lakes
55. Packwood Lake
57. Adams Glacier Camp
62. Gothic Basin
65. Diamond Lake
68. Goat Lake
74. Azurite View
75. Windy Pass
76. Park Butte
80. Cascade Pass
87. Lake Ann
92. Flapjack Lakes
96. Moose Lake
98. Happy Four Shelter

OVERNIGHT HIKES

11. Dutch Miller Gap
20. Foss Lakes
21. Surprise Gap
25. Larch Lake
26. Snow Lakes
27. Lake Caroline
31. Deep Lake
32. Marmot Lake
42. Mystic Lake
54. Shoe Lake
56. Snowgrass Flat
58. Mount Margaret
66. Kennedy Ridge
69. Image Lake
71. Buck Creek Pass
78. Monogram Lake
83. Meadow Cabin
93. Upper Lena Lake
97. High Divide
99. Cape Alava
100. Toleak Point

HIKES OF THREE DAYS OR MORE

26. Enchantment Lakes
28. Lake Mary
70. Lyman Basin
72. Entiat Meadows
73. Park Creek Pass
81. Stehekin to Cascade Pass
99. Rialto Beach-Cape Alava
100. Third Beach-Hoh River

TIME OF YEAR WHEN TRAILS ARE GENERALLY SNOW-FREE

Snow conditions vary each year and patches of snow can be expected at upper elevations for at least a month after the trails are usable. At elevations of over 5000 feet, expect occasional snowstorms even in July and August and frequent snowstorms in September and October. However, these early snowfalls usually melt in a day or two and trails are sometimes usable into early November. High lakes are often snow covered even though the trails are open.

YEAR AROUND

89. Wiley Slough

90. Ayres Point to Dewatto
99. Rialto Beach-Cape Alava

100. Third Beach-Hoh River

OCCASIONALLY SNOWBOUND

1. Tiger Mountain
2. Mt. Si (last mile covered until late April)

14. Wallace Falls
48. Mt. Pete

98. Happy Four Shelter

SNOW-FREE IN APRIL

18. Barclay Lake

83. Middle Cabin

93. Lower Lena Lake

SNOW-FREE IN MAY

16. Heybrook Lookout
29. Davis Peak
30. Paddy-Go-Easy Pass

34. Red Top Mountain
55. Packwood Lake
58. Cedar Creek Camp

66. Kennedy Hot Springs
82. Antenna Station
94. Mt. Jupiter (first three miles)

SNOW-FREE IN JUNE

4. Annette Lake
5. Granite Mountain
6. Pratt Lake
9. Commonwealth Basin
10. Snoqualmie Lake
12. Mount Margaret
13. Rampart Ridge*
15. Lake Serene*

20. Trout Lake
21. Surprise Lake
24. Alpine Lookout
31. Deep Lake*
32. Hyas Lake
33. Long's Pass
35. Bertha May Lakes
37. Gobblers Knob
49. Norse Peak

51. Mount Aix
52. Blankenship Meadows
58. Coldwater Lookout
68. Goat Lake
72. Entiat Meadows
74. Grasshopper Pass
75. Windy Pass
77. Sauk Mountain

*Rampart Lakes, Lake Serene, and Deep Lake may still be covered with snow until July.

SNOW-FREE IN JULY

3. McClellan Butte
7. Melakwa Lake
8. Snow Lake
10. Bear Lake
11. Dutch Miller Gap
12. Lake Lillian
17. Lake Blanca
19. Evergreen Mountain
20. Foss Lakes
21. Surprise Gap
22. Lake Josephine
23. Lake Valhalla
25. Larch Lake
26. Enchantment Lakes
27. Lake Caroline
28. Lake Mary
32. Marmot Lake
35. High Rock Lookout
36. Indian Henrys
38. Emerald Ridge

39. Klapatche Park
42. Moraine Park
43. Tolmie Peak
44. Spray Park
45. Summerland
46. Burroughs Mountain
47. Naches Peak
50. Sourdough Gap
53. Cougar Lakes
54. Shoe Lake
56. Snowgrass Flat
57. Adams Glacier Camp
58. Mount Margaret
59. Mount Pilchuck
60. Mount Forgotten
61. Mount Dickerman
62. Gothic Basin
63. Poodle Dog Pass
64. Glacier Basin
65. Meadow Mountain

66. Kennedy Ridge
69. Image Lake
70. Lyman Basin
71. Buck Creek Pass
76. Park Butte
78. Lookout Mountain
79. Hidden Lake Peaks
80. Cascade Pass
81. Stehekin to
    Cascade Pass
83. Meadow Cabin
84. Coleman Glacier
85. Kulshan Cabin
91. Mount Ellinor
92. Flapjack Lakes
93. Upper Lena Lake
94. Mount Jupiter
95. Lake Constance
96. Moose Lake
97. High Divide

SNOW-FREE MID-JULY OR AUGUST

40. Pinnacle Saddle
41. Paradise Ice Caves

67. Mount Pugh
73. Park Creek Pass
86. Winchester Mountain

87. Lake Ann
88. Table Mountain Loop*

*The trail over the top of Table Mountain may not be usable until late August.

INDEX TO GOVERNMENT MAPS

U. S. 10	FOREST SERVICE TRAIL NO.	FOREST SERVICE MAP	TOPOGRAPHIC OR PLANIMETRIC MAPS
1. Tiger Mountain	State Forest Road		Fall City 7½ min., Hobart 7½ min.
2. Mount Si	State Forest Trail		Bandera 15 min., Mount Si 15 min., Snoqualmie 30 min., and North Bend 30 min.
3. McClellan Butte	1015	North Bend Ranger District (no trail shown)	Bandera 15 min. (no trail shown)
4. Annette Lake	1019	North Bend Ranger District	Snoqualmie Pass 15 min.
5. Granite Mountain	1007 and 1016	North Bend Ranger District	Snoqualmie Pass 15 min.
6. Pratt Lake	1007	North Bend Ranger District	Snoqualmie Pass 15 min. and Bandera 15 min.
7. Melakwa Lake	1014	North Bend Ranger District	Snoqualmie Pass 15 min.
8. Snow Lake	1013	North Bend Ranger District	Snoqualmie Pass 15 min.
9. Commonwealth Basin	2000	North Bend Ranger District	Snoqualmie Pass 15 min.
10. Snoqualmie Basin	1002	North Bend Ranger District	Skykomish No. 3 planimetric
11. Dutch Miller Gap	2133 or 2000	North Bend Ranger District	Skykomish No. 3 and No. 4 planimetric
12. Lake Lillian		Cle Elum Ranger District (no trail shown)	Snoqualmie Pass 15 min.
13. Rampart Ridge	1313	Cle Elum Ranger District	Snoqualmie Pass 15 min.

STEVENS PASS

14. Wallace Falls	State Forest Trail	Skykomish Ranger Ristrict (no trail shown)	Index 15 min.
15. Lake Serene		Skykomish Ranger Ristrict (no trail shown)	Index 15 min.
16. Heybrook Lookout	F. S. Road	Skykomish Ranger District	Index 15 min. and Skykomish No. 2 planimetric
17. Lake Blanca	1052	Skykomish Ranger District	Skykomish No. 2 planimetric
18. Barclay Lake	1055	Skykomish Ranger District	Skykomish No. 2 planimetric
19. Evergreen Mountain	1056	Skykomish Ranger District	Skykomish No. 2 planimetric
20. Foss Lakes	1064	Skykomish Ranger District	Skykomish No. 3 planimetric
21. Surprise Lake	1060 and 2000	Skykomish Ranger District	Skykomish No. 4 planimetric
22. Lake Josephine	2177 or 2000	Skykomish or Leavenworth Ranger Districts	Skykomish No. 4 planimetric
23. Lake Valhalla	2177 or 2000	Skykomish or Leavenworth Ranger Districts	Old Skykomish 30 min. (no trail shown)
24. Alpine Lookout	1583	Leavenworth or Lake Wenatchee Ranger Districts (trail from road to top of ridge not shown)	Chiwaukum No. 2 planimetric

STEVENS PASS (Cont'd)	FOREST SERVICE TRAIL NO.	FOREST SERVICE MAP	TOPOGRAPHIC OR PLANIMETRIC MAPS
25. Larch Lake	1571 and 1573	Leavenworth or Lake Wenatchee Ranger Districts	Chiwaukum No. 3 Planimetric
26. Enchantment Lakes	1553	Leavenworth Ranger District	Chiwaukum 30 min., Mount Stuart 15 min., and Liberty 15 min.
27. Lake Caroline	1554	Leavenworth Ranger District	Chiwaukum No. 3 planimetric
28. Lake Mary	1551 and 1592	Leavenworth Ranger District	Chiwaukum No. 3 planimetric

CLE ELUM

29. Davis Peak	1324	Cle Elum Ranger District	Kachess Lake 15 min.
30. Paddy-Go-Easy Pass	1595	Cle Elum Ranger District	Skykomish No. 4 planimetric
31. Deep Lake	2000 or 2173, 1344 and 1327	Cle Elum Ranger District	Skykomish No. 4 planimetric
32. Marmot Lake	2000 or 2173, and 1066	Cle Elum or Skykomish Ranger Districts	Skykomish No. 4 planimetric
33. Long's Pass		Cle Elum or Leavenworth Ranger Districts (trail not shown on all maps)	Mount Stuart 15 min. (pass shown but not labeled)
34. Red Top Mountain	1364	Ellensburg Ranger District	Mount Stuart 15 min. and Liberty 15 min.

MOUNT RAINIER

35. Bertha May Lakes		Mineral Ranger District	Randle 15 min.
36. Indian Henrys		National Park Rec. Guide	Mount Rainier National Park
37. Gobblers Knob		National Park Rec. Guide	Mount Rainier National Park
38. Emerald Ridge		National Park Rec. Guide	Mount Rainier National Park
39. Klapatche Park		National Park Rec. Guide	Mount Rainier National Park
40. Pinnacle Saddle		National Park Rec. Guide	Mount Rainier National Park
41. Paradise Ice Caves		National Park Rec. Guide	Mount Rainier National Park
42. Moraine Park		National Park Rec. Guide	Mount Rainier National Park
43. Tolmie Peak		National Park Rec. Guide	Mount Rainier National Park
44. Spray Park		National Park Rec. Guide	Mount Rainier National Park
45. Summerland		National Park Rec. Guide	Mount Rainier National Park
46. Burroughs Mountain		National Park Rec. Guide	Mount Rainier National Park
47. Naches Peak		White River or Naches Ranger Districts	Mount Rainier National Park and Bumping Lake 15 min.
48. Mount Pete (Pinnacle or Peak)		No Forest Service Map	Enumclaw 15 min.
49. Norse Peak	1191	White River or Naches Ranger Districts	Bumping Lake 15 min.
50. Sourdough Gap	2000	White River or Naches Ranger Districts	Bumping Lake 15 min. and Mount Rainier National Park
51. Mount Aix		Naches Ranger District	Bumping Lake 15 min.
52. Tumac Mountain		Naches Ranger District	White Pass 15 min. and Bumping Lake 15 min.)
53. Cougar Lakes	970 and 958	Naches Ranger District	Bumping Lake 15 min.

SOUTH OF RAINIER	FOREST SERVICE TRAIL NO.	FOREST SERVICE MAP	TOPOGRAPHIC OR PLANIMETRIC MAPS
54. Shoe Lake	44, 1144 or 2000	Packwood Ranger District or Goat Rocks Wild Area Special Folder	White Pass 15 min.
55. Packwood Lake	78	Packwood Ranger District or Goat Rocks Wild Area Special Folder	Packwood 15 min.
56. Snowgrass Flat	96 and 86	Packwood Ranger District or Goat Rocks Wild Area Special Folder	White Pass 15 min., Packwood 15 min., Mount Adams 30 min., and Steamboat Mountain 30 min. (no road shown)
57. Adams Glacier Camp	113	Packwood Ranger District (last mile not shown)	Steamboat Mountain 30 min. (no road shown)
58. Mount Margaret	207 and 211	Packwood Ranger District or Spirit Lake Recreation Guide	Steamboat Mountain 30 min. (no road or trail shown) Spirit Lake 15 min.
MOUNTAIN LOOP AREA			
59. Mount Pilchuck	700	Monte Cristo Ranger District	Granite Falls 15 min.
60. Mount Forgotten	711	Monte Cristo Ranger District	Glacier Peak No. 3 planimetric and Silverton 15 min.
61. Mount Dickerman		Monte Cristo Ranger District (no trail shown)	Glacier Peak No. 3 planimetric
62. Gothic Basin		Monte Cristo Ranger District (no trail shown)	Skykomish No. 2 planimetric (no trail shown) and Glacier Peak No. 3 planimetric
63. Poodle Dog Pass	708	Monte Cristo Ranger District	Skykomish No. 2 planimetric
64. Glacier Basin		Monte Cristo Ranger District (no trail shown)	Skykomish No. 2 planimetric (no trail shown)
65. Meadow Mountain	657	Suiattle Ranger District	Glacier Peak No. 3 planimetric
66. Kennedy Ridge	643 and 2056	Suiattle Ranger District	Glacier Peak 15 min. and Glacier Peak No. 3 planimetric
67. Mount Pugh	644	Suiattle Ranger District	Glacier Peak No. 3 planimetric
68. Goat Lake	647	Suiattle Ranger District	Glacier Peak No. 3 planimetric
69. Image Lake	784 and 785	Suiattle Ranger District	Glacier Peak 15 min. and Holden 15 min.
70. Lyman Basin	784 or 2000 and 1256	Suiattle and Entiat Ranger Districts	Glacier Peak 15 min. and Holden 15 min. (Lucerne 15 min. shows road)
EAST SLOPE			
71. Buck Creek Pass	1513	Entiat or Lake Wenatchee Ranger Districts	Holden 15 min.
72. Entiat Meadows	1400 and 1405	Entiat Ranger District	Lucerne 15 min. and Holden 15 min.
73. Park Creek Pass	1270	Chelan Ranger District	Goode Mountain 7½ min.
74. Grasshopper Pass		Pasayten Ranger District	Slate Peak 7½ min.
75. Windy Pass		Pasayten Ranger District	Slate Peak 7½ min. and Ptarmigan Peak planimetric

NORTH CASCADES	FOREST SERVICE TRAIL NO.	FOREST SERVICE MAP	TOPOGRAPHIC PLANIMETRIC MAPS
76. Park Butte	601	Baker River Ranger Ristrict	Hamilton, Washington, 15 min. (no road shown)
77. Sauk Mountain	613	Baker River Ranger Ristrict	Lake Shannon, 15 min. (incomplete road)
78. Lookout Mountain	743	Skagit Ranger Dist. (no trail shown to Monogram Lake)	Marblemount 15 min. (no trail to lake shown)
79. Hidden Lake Peaks	745	Skagit Ranger District	Eldorado Peak 7½ min. and Sonny Boy Lakes 7½ min.
80. Sahale Arm	744	Skagit Ranger Dist. (no trail shown to Sahale Arm)	Cascade Pass 7½ min.
81. Stehekin to Cascade Pass	1234 and 744	Suiattle, Darrington, and Monte Cristo Ranger Districts	Cascade Pass 7½ min., Goode Mountain 7½ min., McGregor 7½ min., Mount Lyall 7½ min., and Stehekin No. 1 planimetric
82. Sourdough Mountain	739	Skagit Ranger District	Diablo Dam 7½ min. and Ross Dam 7½ min.
83. Thunder Creek	740	Skagit Ranger District	Ross Dam 7½ min. and Forbidden Peak 7½ min.
84. Coleman Glacier		Glacier Ranger District (no trail shown)	Mount Baker 15 min. (no trail shown)
85. Kulshan Cabin	677	Glacier Ranger District	Mount Baker 15 min.
86. Winchester Mountain	685	Glacier Ranger District	Mount Shuksan 15 min.
87. Lake Ann	600	Glacier Ranger District	Mount Shuksan 15 min.
88. Table Mountain	682 and 681	Glacier Ranger District	Mount Shuksan 15 min.

BEACH WALKS

90. Ayres Point to Dewatto			Potlatch 15 min.

OLYMPIC MOUNTAINS

91. Mount Ellinor	812	Hoodsport Ranger District	Mount Steele 15 min. and The Brothers 15 min.
92. Flapjack Lakes		Hoodsport Ranger District	Mount Steele 15 min.
93. Upper Lena Lake		Hoodsport Ranger District	The Brothers, 15 min.
94. Mount Jupiter	809	Hoodsport Ranger District	The Brothers 15 min. and Point Misery 15 min.
95. Lake Constance		Hoodsport Ranger District	Tyler Peak 15 min. and The Brothers 15 min.
96. Moose Lake			Mount Angeles 15 min.
97. High Divide			Mount Tom 15 min. and Mount Olympus 15 min.
98. Happy Four Shelter			Mount Tom 15 min.
99. Rialto Beach-Cape Alava			Ozette 15 min. and LaPush 15 min.
100. Third Beach-Hoh River			LaPush 15 min., Forks 15 min., and Destruction Island 15 min.

HOW TO ACQUIRE MAPS

Forest Service maps are given free at Ranger Stations or by writing Forest Supervisors.

BAKER NATIONAL FOREST
Write: **Forest Supervisor**
U. S. Forest Service
Bellingham, Washington 98225

1. Suiattle, Darrington, and Monte Cristo Ranger Districts
2. Glacier, Baker River, and Skagit Ranger Districts

WENATCHEE NATIONAL FOREST
Write: **Forest Supervisor**
U. S. Forest Service
P.O. Box 811
Wenatchee, Washington

1. Leavenworth, Cashmere Ranger Districts
2. Entiat, Chelan Ranger Districts
3. Lake Wenatchee Ranger District
4. Cle Elum Ranger District
5. Ellensburg Ranger District

GIFFORD PINCHOT NATIONAL FOREST
Write: **Forest Supervisor**
U. S. Forest Service
P.O. Box 449
Vancouver, Washington 98660

1. Spirit Lake, Randle, Packwood, and Mt. Adams Ranger Districts
2. Lewis River, Canyon Creek, Wind River, and Willard Ranger Districts
3. Mt. St. Helens and Spirit Lake Recreation Guide
4. Goat Rocks Recreation Guide

SNOQUALMIE NATIONAL FOREST
Write: **Forest Supervisor**
U. S. Forest Service
905 2nd Avenue Building
Seattle, Washington 98104

1. White River Ranger District
2. North Bend, Skykomish Ranger Districts
3. Mineral Ranger District
4. Naches, Tieton Ranger Districts

OKANOGAN NATIONAL FOREST
Write: **Forest Supervisor**
U. S. Forest Service
P.O. Box 432
Okanogan, Washington 98840

1. Winthrop Ranger District
2. Pasayten Ranger District

OLYMPIC NATIONAL FOREST
Write: **Forest Supervisor**
U. S. Forest Service
P.O. Box 187
Olympia, Washington 98502

1. Quilcene and Hoodsport Ranger Districts
2. Forks Ranger District

PLANIMETRIC MAPS
Planimetric maps — 1 inch scale can be ordered from: **Survey and Map Section**
U. S. Forest Service
P.O. Box 3623
Portland, Oregon 97208

Order by name and number of map from chart "Status of Planimetric Mapping" given free at the above Forest Service address.
1 inch scale maps, 45c each

Payment should be made in exact amount payable to the U. S. Forest Service and included with the order.

NATIONAL PARK MAPS
National Park maps are free, write to Superintendent of each park:

Mount Rainier National Park,
Longmire, Washington 98397

Olympic National Park,
Port Angeles, Washington 98362

TOPOGRAPHIC MAPS
Topographic maps can be obtained at local map stores and stores specializing in hiking and climbing equipment.

Advance copies of unreleased maps are available (50c each) from: **U. S. Geological Survey Office**
345 Middlefield Road
Menlo Park, California